THE FIFTH JUDICIAL CIRCUIT
OF ILLINOIS

THE FIFTH JUDICIAL CIRCUIT OF ILLINOIS

JAMES R. GLENN

Order this book online at www.trafford.com
or email orders@trafford.com

Most Trafford titles are also available at major online book retailers.

Printed in the United States of America.

ISBN: 978-1-4269-5199-2 (sc)
ISBN: 978-1-4269-5200-5 (e)

Trafford rev. 02/17/2011

 www.trafford.com

North America & international
toll-free: 1 888 232 4444 (USA & Canada)
phone: 250 383 6864 ♦ fax: 812 355 4082

Contents

I
EARLY YEARS

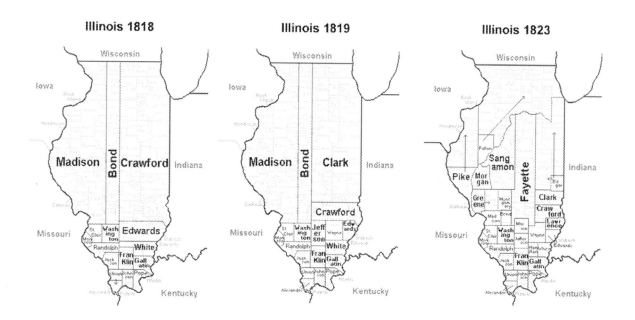

Illinois became a state on December 3, 1818. It consisted of fifteen counties, including Crawford, which comprised all of the area north of Edwards County and east of Bond County.[1] Clark County assumed much of that immense area upon its creation on March 22, 1819,[2] as did Edgar County, when it was created on January 3, 1823.[3] Vermilion County separated from Edgar County on January 18, 1826.[4] On December 25, 1830, Coles County, which included within its borders present day Cumberland and Douglas Counties, was created from the western portions of Clark and Edgar Counties.[5] Cumberland County was established on March 2, 1843.[6]

---

[1] Michael L. Hebert, "Illinois 1818," Illinois County Boundaries 1790-Present. http://maps.ilgw.org/il1818.htm.
[2] Michael L. Hebert, "Illinois 1819," Illinois County Boundaries 1790-Present. http://maps.ilgw.org/il1819.htm.
[3] Michael L. Hebert, "Illinois 1823," Illinois County Boundaries 1790-Present. http://maps.ilgw.org/il1823.htm.
[4] Michael L. Hebert, "Illinois 1826," Illinois County Boundaries 1790-Present. http://maps.ilgw.org/il1826.htm.
[5] Michael L. Hebert, "Illinois 1831," Illinois County Boundaries 1790-Present. http://maps.ilgw.org/il1831.htm.
[6] Michael L. Hebert, "Illinois 1843," Illinois County Boundaries 1790-Present. http://maps.ilgw.org/il1843.htm.

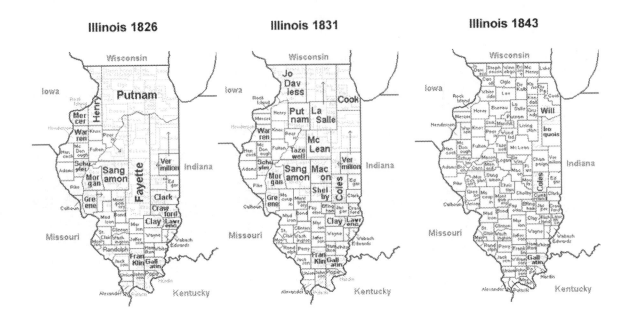

The constitution of the new state provided for a supreme court of four justices, appointed by the General Assembly. Although the Supreme Court had appellate jurisdiction in most cases, its justices were required to individually ride the various circuits.[7] The first term of the local Circuit Court convened on September 20, 1819 in Aurora, the first county seat of Clark County, located approximately two miles north of Darwin. Supreme Court Justice Thomas C. Browne presided. Shortly thereafter, Supreme Court Justice William Wilson began appearing in Clark County,[8] which was initially part of the Second Judicial District.[9] Wilson, who was only twenty-five years of age when appointed,[10] served on the Supreme Court from 1819 to 1848.[11] His time in Clark County was not spent entirely in Aurora. The seat of the county's government moved to Darwin on January 21, 1823 and then to Marshall in 1838.[12]

On December 29, 1824, Illinois was divided into five circuits, the judges of which were elected by the General Assembly and commissioned on January 19, 1825.[13] Clark and Edgar Counties became part of the Fifth Circuit,[14] with James O. Wattles holding office as

---

[7] David F. Rolewick, *A Short History of the Illinois Judicial Systems* (Springfield: Administrative Office of the Illinois Courts, 1971), 8; Ill. Const. of 1818 art. IV, secs. 2, 3, 4.

[8] H. C. Bell, ed., *Clark County* (Chicago: Middle West Publishing Co., 1907), 622, 629, 630.

[9] 1819 Ill. Laws 157.

[10] John Twomey, ed., *Vermilion County Bench and Bar: The First One Hundred Fifty Years 1826-1976* (Danville: The Vermilion County Bar Association, 1977), 19.

[11] William J. Stratton, ed., *Blue Book of the State of Illinois, 1931-1932* (Springfield: Journal Printing Co., 1931), 679.

[12] Bell, ed., *Clark County*, 625, 626.

[13] Stratton, ed., *Blue Book of the State of Illinois, 1931-1932*, 682.

[14] 1824 Ill. Laws 42.

the first circuit judge.[15] Vermilion County became part of that circuit upon its creation.[16] However, on January 12, 1827, the circuit judges were legislated out of existence and the Supreme Court justices were again required to hold court in the circuits.[17] Clark, Edgar, and Vermilion Counties were placed in the Fourth Circuit.[18]

The state legislature had provided on March 23, 1819 that a resident would be appointed in each circuit as "circuit attorney" to handle prosecutions.[19] That title changed to "state's attorney" on February 19, 1827.[20] William Wilson briefly served as the circuit attorney for the Second Judicial District in 1819, prior to his appointment to the Supreme Court, but he never had an opportunity to prosecute cases in Clark County.[21] John M. Robinson held the circuit and state's attorney position during the 1820's. He then served in the United States Senate from 1830 to 1841[22] and on the Illinois Supreme Court from March 6, 1843 until his death on April 27, 1843.[23]

In 1819, the General Assembly established justice of the peace courts, where two or more justices presided in each of two or more districts in every county.[24] Courts of probate began operation on May 1, 1821.[25] Until then, county affairs were managed by county commissioners' courts.[26] On April 26, 1819, Joseph Shaw, John Chenoweth, and Samuel Ashmore were elected Clark County's first commissioners. William B. Archer was appointed the first clerk of the County Commissioners' Court on June 7, 1819,[27] but held the office only until 1820.[28] The first judge of probate in 1821 was Samuel Prevo.[29] The title of the position became probate justice of the peace on August 7, 1837.[30]

On January 7, 1835, the General Assembly again provided for circuit judges.[31] Coles County had already joined Clark, Edgar, and Vermilion Counties in the Fourth Circuit,[32] for which Justin Harlan became the new circuit judge.[33] In 1841, however, the circuit judges were once again removed,[34] and Supreme Court Justice Wilson resumed duties in the Fourth

[15] Bell, ed., *Clark County*, 630.

[16] 1826 Ill. Laws 52.

[17] Rolewick, *A Short History of the Illinois Judicial Systems*, 8.

[18] 1827 Ill. Laws 118-119.

[19] 1819 Ill. Laws 204.

[20] 1827 Ill. Laws 79.

[21] William H. Perrin, ed., *History of Crawford and Clark Counties, Illinois* (Chicago: O. L. Baskin & Co., 1883), 47.

[22] *Illinois Biographical Dictionary* (New York: Somerset Publishers, Inc., 1993), 300.

[23] Stratton, ed., *Blue Book of the State of Illinois, 1931-1932*, 679.

[24] Rolewick, *A Short History of the Illinois Judicial Systems*, 10.

[25] 1821 Ill. Laws 119-126.

[26] Perrin, ed., *History of Crawford and Clark Counties, Illinois*, 247.

[27] Bell, ed., *Clark County*, 622.

[28] Perrin, ed., *History of Crawford and Clark Counties, Illinois*, 256.

[29] Bell, ed., *Clark County*, 633.

[30] 1837 Ill. Laws 176-178.

[31] Stratton, ed., *Blue Book of the State of Illinois, 1931-1932*, 683.

[32] 1831 Ill. Laws 45.

[33] Stratton, ed., *Blue Book of the State of Illinois, 1931-1932*, 683.

[34] Rolewick, *A Short History of the Illinois Judicial Systems*, 10.

Circuit. Edgar and Vermilion Counties moved to the Eighth Circuit on February 21, 1845,[35] where Supreme Court Justice Samuel H. Treat presided.[36] Newly formed Cumberland County became part of the Fourth Circuit,[37] and had Greenup as its initial seat of justice. Prairie City, later known as Toledo, became the county seat in 1855.[38] The circuit continued to be represented by ambitious state's attorneys. Orlando B. Ficklin, Aaron Shaw, and Augustus C. French each prosecuted cases in the 1830's. Ficklin and Shaw later served in Congress, while French became governor of the State of Illinois. Garland B. Shelledy of Paris held office from 1839 to 1841, prior to Shaw's second term.[39]

In 1848, a new constitution was drafted and adopted. It provided that circuit judges would be elected in September, 1848, in June, 1855, and then every six years thereafter. State's attorneys, once again limited to one per circuit, would also be elected in September, 1848, but then in November, 1852 and every four years thereafter. The constitution also created county courts.[40] The county judges of those courts assumed the duties of the former probate justices of the peace and were elected in November, 1849 and every four years thereafter.[41] The counties continued to utilize justices of the peace,[42] while the General Assembly temporarily provided for two associate justices in each county to sit with the county judge in all cases.[43]

Harlan returned to the position of circuit judge of the Fourth Circuit, defeating retiring Supreme Court Justice Wilson in the September 4, 1848 election. David Davis was elected in the Eighth Circuit[44] and reelected, along with Harlan, in 1855.[45] Davis was appointed to the Supreme Court of the United States by President Abraham Lincoln in 1862, where he served until 1877.[46] He was later elected to the United States Senate.[47]

The legislature made several changes in the composition of judicial circuits. Edgar County moved from the Eighth to the Fourth Circuit on February 12, 1853.[48] Coles County moved to the Seventeenth Circuit on February 12, 1857[49] and back to the Fourth Circuit on February 1, 1859.[50] On February 4, 1861, the Twenty-Seventh Circuit, which included

---

[35] 1845 Ill. Laws 47.

[36] Stratton, ed., *Blue Book of the State of Illinois, 1931-1932*, 683.

[37] 1843 Ill. Laws 94-98, 134.

[38] *Counties of Cumberland, Jasper and Richland, Illinois* (Chicago: F. A. Battey & Co., 1884), 93, 136, 217.

[39] Bell, ed., *Clark County*, 637, 638.

[40] Ill. Const. of 1848 art. V, secs. 13, 15, 16, 21, 28.

[41] 1849 Ill. Laws 62.

[42] Ill. Const. of 1848 art. V, sec. 27.

[43] Rolewick, *A Short History of the Illinois Judicial Systems*, 11.

[44] State of Illinois Secretary of State, *Abstract of Election Returns 1818-1850*, 582-583.

[45] State of Illinois Secretary of State, *Abstract of Election Returns 1850-1862*, 125-126.

[46] Twomey, ed., *Vermilion County Bench and Bar: The First One Hundred Fifty Years 1826-1976*, 22.

[47] *Illinois Biographical Dictionary*, 107.

[48] 1853 Ill. Laws 64.

[49] 1857 Ill. Laws 19.

[50] 1859 Ill. Laws 52.

Vermilion County, was established.[51] Edgar and Coles Counties joined that circuit on February 10, 1865.[52]

Harlan was defeated for reelection to the circuit bench in 1861 by fellow Clark County resident Charles H. Constable[53] and in 1867 by Hiram B. Decius.[54] Harlan, nevertheless, resurfaced as county judge of Clark County from 1873 to 1877.[55] Decius, formerly a Cumberland County judge, was commissioned on December 1, 1865,[56] after Constable's death on October 9, 1865.[57] During that period, Robert B. Lamon had the distinction of being county judge in two different counties. In 1863, he was elected in Vermilion County to fill an unexpired term.[58] After an unsuccessful reelection bid in 1865, Lamon was elected in Edgar County in 1869 and 1873, before losing the election of 1877.[59] His son, Walter, was Edgar County judge from 1902 to 1910 and later state's attorney for two terms.[60] Andrew J. Hunter, another Edgar County resident, was elected county judge in his home county in 1886 and 1890. Although he was elected to Congress in 1892,[61] Hunter continued to perform his judicial duties until replaced by Henry Tanner in 1894.

The area showcased some state's attorneys of note. Ward H. Lamon held the office in the Eighth Circuit from 1856 to 1861, after which time he followed President Lincoln, his former partner in a Danville law office, to Washington, D.C. There he became a United States marshal.[62] John Scholfield of Marshall held the office of state's attorney in the Fourth Circuit from 1856 to 1860.[63] He later served on the Supreme Court from 1873 until his death on February 13, 1893.[64] Joseph G. Cannon, who in 1860 had been defeated in the Fourth Circuit by future Coles County Judge James R. Cunningham,[65] was state's attorney for the Twenty-Seventh Circuit from 1861 to 1868.[66] He then represented constituents for nearly fifty years as a member of the United States Congress, including from 1903 to 1911 as the powerful speaker of the House.[67] John Boyle of Paris succeeded Cannon in the Twenty-

[51] 1861 Ill. Laws 99.

[52] 1865 Ill. Laws 32.

[53] Newton Bateman and Paul Selby, ed., *Historical Encyclopedia of Illinois* (Chicago: Munsell Publishing Co., for Middle-West Publishing Co., 1906), 117.

[54] State of Illinois Secretary of State, *Abstract of Election Returns 1850-1862*, 320; State of Illinois Secretary of State, *Abstract of Election Returns 1862-1873*, 166.

[55] State of Illinois Secretary of State, *Abstract of Election Returns 1873-1882*, 20.

[56] Stratton, ed., *Blue Book of the State of Illinois, 1931-1932*, 683.

[57] Perrin, ed., *History of Crawford and Clark Counties, Illinois*, 291.

[58] *The History of Edgar County, Illinois* (Chicago: Wm. Le Baron, Jr. & Co., 1879), 584.

[59] State of Illinois Secretary of State, *Abstract of Election Returns 1862-1873*, 126, 254; State of Illinois Secretary of State, *Abstract of Election Returns 1873-1882*, 22, 178.

[60] H. Van Sellar, ed., *History of Edgar County* (Chicago: Munsell Publishing Co., 1905), 736.

[61] Ibid., 730.

[62] Twomey, ed., *Vermilion County Bench and Bar: The First One Hundred Fifty Years 1826-1976*, 8.

[63] Bell, ed., *Clark County*, 635.

[64] Stratton, ed., *Blue Book of the State of Illinois, 1931-1932*, 679.

[65] State of Illinois Secretary of State, *Abstract of Election Returns 1850-1862*, 272.

[66] "Cannon, Joseph Gurney, (1836-1926)," Biographical Directory of the United States Congress 1774-Present. http://bioguide.congress.gov/scripts/biodisplay.pl?index=c000121.

[67] Twomey, ed., *Vermilion County Bench and Bar: The First One Hundred Fifty Years 1826-1976*, 11.

Seventh Circuit.[68] Boyle's term was completed by Charleston's Alexander P. Dunbar, who took office in 1870.[69]

Silas Whitehead of Marshall was state's attorney for the Fourth Circuit from 1864 to 1872. On June 9, 1877, Whitehead shot and killed his successor, Clark County State's Attorney John L. Ryan. The shooting was the result of a fight between the two men at a time when Attorney Whitehead was defending a man before a justice of the peace for cutting Ryan with a knife. Whitehead was initially convicted and sentenced to a year in prison. A new trial was ordered, however, and Whitehead was acquitted.[70]

Due to the great population increases in Illinois during the 1850's and 1860's, more courts were established. In 1854, the General Assembly created the position of police magistrate for towns and cities, the numbers of which would be based on population. The jurisdiction of the police magistrate courts was similar to that of the justice of the peace courts, but neither were courts of record. As a result, appeals to courts of record, such as the county court or circuit court, became trials *de novo*, or new trials. Some growing cities eased the situation by establishing courts of common pleas, which had jurisdiction concurrent with that of the circuit courts.[71] Mattoon established a common pleas court on March 6, 1869, although it was not a court of record. William W. Craddock was elected the first justice. The purpose of the local court was to eliminate travel to Charleston, but because appeals were taken to the Circuit Court in Charleston, travel actually increased. Accordingly, Mattoon's Court of Common Pleas dissolved on April 29, 1873.[72]

Another constitution was adopted in 1870. It maintained six-year terms for circuit judges and four-year terms for county judges, but provided for a state's attorney in each county, beginning in 1872.[73] It also established an appellate court, which consisted of at least three judges in each of four districts, assigned from the circuit courts by the Supreme Court.[74] The county judges continued to be elected in odd-numbered years through the election of November 6, 1877. However, future elections took place in November, 1882 and every four years thereafter.[75]

On March 28, 1873, the legislature divided the state, exclusive of Cook County, into twenty-six judicial circuits, each electing one judge. Clark, Edgar, Vermilion, and Coles Counties became part of the Fifteenth Circuit,[76] which elected Danville's Oliver L. Davis its circuit judge. Davis had previously served in the Twenty-Seventh Circuit from 1861

---

[68] Charles Edward Wilson, ed., *History of Coles County* (Chicago: Munsell Publishing Co., 1906), 677.

[69] *The History of Coles County, Illinois* (Chicago: Wm. Le Baron, Jr. & Co., 1879), 518.

[70] Bell, ed., *Clark County*, 638-639.

[71] Rolewick, *A Short History of the Illinois Judicial Systems*, 11-12.

[72] *History of the City of Mattoon, Illinois*, 44, 45, 51, 53; 1873 Ill. Laws 82-83.

[73] Ill. Const. of 1870 art. VI, secs. 12, 18, 22.

[74] Rolewick, *A Short History of the Illinois Judicial Systems*, 13-15.

[75] 1881 Ill. Laws 70.

[76] 1873 Ill. Laws 106.

to 1866,[77] where he was succeeded by former Edgar County Judge James Steele,[78] whom Davis defeated in the 1873 election.[79] Cumberland County became part of the Twenty-First Circuit,[80] where James C. Allen of Palestine was elected circuit judge. Both Davis and Allen were among the first judges assigned to the Appellate Court in September, 1877.[81]

In 1877, the General Assembly combined the circuits outside of Cook County, reducing their number to thirteen, but provided for the election in each circuit of another circuit judge, raising the number of judges in each circuit to three. The counties of the Fifteenth and Sixteenth Circuits, in which Davis and Champaign's Charles B. Smith presided, were placed in the Fourth Circuit.[82] William E. Nelson of Decatur became the third circuit judge, but left office in 1879, when Davis, Smith, and Marshall's Jacob W. Wilkin were elected. Smith spent time with the Appellate Court.[83] Wilkin was the son-in-law of former Fourth Circuit Judge Charles H. Constable.[84] After his reelection in 1885 and designation to the Appellate Court, Wilkin was elected to the Supreme Court, where he operated from 1888 until his death on April 4, 1907.[85]

Cumberland County and the other counties of the Twenty-First and Twenty-Fourth Circuits became the Second Circuit.[86] John H. Halley of Newton joined Allen and Mt. Vernon's Tazewell B. Tanner on the circuit bench in 1877, but all were replaced in 1879, when Chauncey S. Conger of Carmi, Thomas S. Casey of Mt. Vernon, and William C. Jones of Robinson were elected. Tanner, Conger, and Casey also spent time with the Appellate Court. Carroll C. Boggs of Fairfield, who succeeded Casey in 1885, served not only on the Appellate Court, but also on the Supreme Court.[87]

Two close elections occurred in state's attorneys races on November 8, 1892. In Coles County, incumbent State's Attorney John H. Marshall appeared to be victorious over his Democratic Party challenger, John S. Hall, 3,653 to 3,648. Jackson A. Colby of both the Prohibition and People's Parties tallied 269 votes. A canvass of returns, however, resulted in totals of 3,652 votes for Hall and 3,648 for Marshall.[88] Hall filed a contest of election against Marshall on December 5, 1892 in the Coles County Court. The trial, during which the ballots were recounted, commenced on January 20, 1893 before Judge Lapsley C. Henley. On February 10, 1893, the Court declared Marshall the winner, finding that he had 3,652

[77] Stratton, ed., *Blue Book of the State of Illinois, 1931-1932*, 684, 685.

[78] Van Sellar, ed., *History of Edgar County*, 661.

[79] State of Illinois Secretary of State, *Abstract of Election Returns 1873-1882*, 7.

[80] 1873 Ill. Laws 106.

[81] Stratton, ed., *Blue Book of the State of Illinois, 1931-1932*, 682, 685.

[82] 1877 Ill. Laws 73.

[83] Stratton, ed., *Blue Book of the State of Illinois, 1931-1932*, 681.

[84] Bell, ed., *Clark County*, 630.

[85] Stratton, ed., *Blue Book of the State of Illinois, 1931-1932*, 679, 682, 685.

[86] 1877 Ill. Laws 73.

[87] Stratton, ed., *Blue Book of the State of Illinois, 1931-1932*, 680, 682, 685.

[88] State of Illinois Secretary of State, *Abstract of Election Returns 1882-1912*, 268.

votes, while Hall had only 3,611. Marshall later served as a circuit judge from 1915 until his death in 1927.[89]

In Edgar County, the contest between Democratic Party candidate Alfred Tanner and his Republican opponent, Willis H. Clinton, finished in a tie, as the two frontrunners each accumulated 3,173 votes. John F. Boyer of the People's Party received 180 votes, while Prohibition candidate Dillard N. Johnson took 150. Although Clinton alleged in a mandamus proceeding that precinct tally sheets showed five more votes for him and five less votes for Tanner, the canvassing board found the result of the election to be deadlocked. Therefore, on November 16, 1892, Tanner and Clinton both appeared at the county clerk's office for the drawing of lots. Two toothpicks were used, one of which had a piece bitten off. When Tanner pulled the longer toothpick, he became Edgar County's state's attorney-elect. Clinton did not pursue his petition for a writ of mandamus.[90]

---

[89] Stratton, ed., *Blue Book of the State of Illinois, 1931-1932*, 687.
[90] *The Paris Daily Beacon*, November 17, 1892, 1, 4.

II

FIFTH CIRCUIT

On April 23, 1897, the General Assembly approved an act which divided the State of Illinois, exclusive of Cook County, into seventeen judicial circuits. That legislation gave birth to the Fifth Circuit, which has consisted ever since of Clark, Coles, Cumberland, Edgar, and Vermilion Counties.[1] On June 7, 1897, the first three judges of the Fifth Circuit were elected, all Republicans: Henry Van Sellar of Paris, Frank K. Dunn of Charleston, and Ferdinand Bookwalter of Danville. Bookwalter had already been serving as a circuit judge in the Fourth Circuit. He died in 1902 and was succeeded on September 17 of that year by Morton W. Thompson, the county judge of Vermilion County. Dunn was later a justice of the Supreme Court from 1907 to 1933.[2]

In 1903, much to the chagrin of area Republicans, Dunn was not renominated for the circuit bench. Although the majority of Fifth Circuit voters were Republican, Democrats E. R. E. Kimbrough of Danville and James W. Craig of Mattoon, a former Coles County state's attorney, were the top vote getters in the judicial election of 1903, followed by Thompson.[3] The defeat of Van Sellar and Marshall's Fenton W. Booth was viewed by some as an angry reaction to the absence of Dunn on the ballot.[4] Kimbrough and Thompson were reelected in 1909. Craig did not run,[5] but the Democratic Party retained the position, as Marshall's William B. Scholfield, the son of former Supreme Court Justice John Scholfield[6] and later an appellate judge himself, prevailed.[7] The Republican Party regained control of the Circuit Court in 1915 with the election of future Appellate Court assignee Augustus A. Partlow of Danville, Cumberland County State's Attorney Walter Brewer of Toledo, and John H.

---

[1] 1897 Ill. Laws 188.
[2] Stratton, ed., *Blue Book of the State of Illinois, 1931-1932*, 680, 685, 687.
[3] State of Illinois Secretary of State, *Abstract of Election Returns 1882-1912*, 410-411.
[4] Bell, ed., *Clark County*, 632.
[5] Stratton, ed., *Blue Book of the State of Illinois, 1931-1932*, 687.
[6] Bell, ed., *Clark County*, 640, 645.
[7] Stratton, ed., *Blue Book of the State of Illinois, 1931-1932*, 682, 687.

Marshall of Charleston,[8] all of whom were unopposed for reelection in 1921.[9] Republican judges dominated the three circuit slots for a period of eighteen years.

In addition to the Circuit Court and county courts, the Fifth Circuit consisted of two city courts and a probate court. The jurisdiction of a city court was primarily concurrent with that of a circuit court.[10] Mattoon established its city court in 1897 and elected former Circuit Judge James F. Hughes as its first city judge on January 25, 1898.[11] Charleston created its city court in 1910 and elected Charles A. Shuey, who would later become a circuit judge, as its first city judge.[12] Probate courts emerged from the Constitution of 1870 and were permitted in counties of sufficiently large population.[13] Vermilion County began electing probate judges in 1910. Clinton Abernathy was the first.[14]

Like county and probate judges, judges of the city court were originally elected to terms of four years. That changed after 1927, however, when the General Assembly extended the terms to six years.[15] After Hughes, city judges in Mattoon included former County Judge Lapsley C. Henley and former Common Pleas Court Justice Horace S. Clark, who died in office on April 11, 1907.[16] Isaac B. Craig, the brother of Circuit Judge James W. Craig,[17] served from 1922 to 1925, but also died in office.[18] After Shuey, city judges in Charleston included future County Judge John T. Kincaid and future Circuit and Appellate Judge Ben F. Anderson,[19] whose brother, Herbert S. Anderson,[20] was elected in 1930.[21] Herbert's son, Jack H. Anderson, was elected to the position thirty years later.[22]

The circuit experienced two election contests in the 1930's. In the county election of November 4, 1930, Republican Walter J. Bookwalter, the son of Circuit Judge Ferdinand Bookwalter,[23] seemed to be victorious in his bid for a fifth term as probate judge of Vermilion County, outpolling Ralph M. Jinkins 11,701 to 11,518.[24] Oddly, votes were not counted from one of the county's precincts, leading Jinkins to bring mandamus proceedings in the

[8] Ibid., 681, 687.

[9] Louis L. Emmerson, ed., *Blue Book of the State of Illinois, 1921-1922* (Springfield: Illinois State Journal Co., 1921), 832.

[10] Rolewick, *A Short History of the Illinois Judicial Systems*, 16.

[11] *History of the City of Mattoon, Illinois*, 100, 109.

[12] *The Charleston Daily Courier*, September 7, 1910, 1.

[13] Rolewick, *A Short History of the Illinois Judicial Systems*, 16.

[14] Twomey, ed., *Vermilion County Bench and Bar: The First One Hundred Fifty Years 1826-1976*, 32.

[15] 1927 Ill. Laws 390.

[16] *The Mattoon Journal-Gazette*, April 12, 1907, 1.

[17] Craig Van Meter, *The Legal Profession in Coles County* (Charleston: Coles County Historical Society, 1976), 4.

[18] *The Daily Journal-Gazette*, August 4, 1925, 1.

[19] Charles S. Carpentier, ed., *Blue Book of the State of Illinois, 1953-1954* (Springfield: State of Illinois Secretary of State, 1954), 163.

[20] Van Meter, *The Legal Profession in Coles County*, 4.

[21] *The Charleston Daily News*, September 3, 1930, 1.

[22] *The Charleston Courier-News*, July 5, 1960, 1.

[23] Twomey, ed., *Vermilion County Bench and Bar: The First One Hundred Fifty Years 1826-1976*, 9.

[24] State of Illinois Secretary of State, *Abstract of Election Returns 1882-1912*, 279.

Circuit Court,[25] followed by an election contest.[26] Jinkins was successful, as Circuit Judge S. Murray Clark, formerly a county judge of Vermilion County, declared him elected by a majority of 330 votes.[27] Jinkins was reelected in 1934, but lost the elections of 1938 and 1942 to Arthur R. Hall,[28] formerly a part-time football coach at the University of Illinois.[29]

In the Cumberland County primary election of April 14, 1936, Glen D. Neal appeared to edge incumbent Theodore O. Cutright in the Democratic race for state's attorney by a vote of 1,374 to 1,371.[30] Cutright filed a contest of election.[31] After a three-day trial before Coles County Judge John T. Kincaid, Cutright was declared the winner, 1,373-1/2 to 1,371. The fraction was the result of illegal votes, portions of which were subtracted from the totals of both candidates.[32] Cutright was reelected state's attorney in November.[33] Neal later served six terms as Cumberland County state's attorney, longer than any other prosecutor in the Fifth Circuit. Until then, Thomas L. Orndorff of Clark County and John H. Lewman of Vermilion County set the standard with four terms each, with Orndorff holding office during the previous century and Lewman doing so from 1908 to 1924. Lewman's period of service as state's attorney is still the longest in the history of Vermilion County.

As the world was immersed in the Great Depression, the Democratic Party rose to prominence throughout the United States. That development also occurred in the Fifth Circuit. In 1932, all five counties elected Democratic state's attorneys.[34] All but Cumberland County had elected Republicans to that office in 1928, and three of those incumbents were defeated in 1932.[35] In 1933, incumbent Republican Circuit Judges Clark and Shuey were defeated by Democrats Craig Van Meter of Mattoon and Casper Platt of Danville.[36] Shuey had won a special election in 1927, after the death of John H. Marshall.[37] Van Meter, the grandson of James W. Craig,[38] served less than three years, resigning on January 1, 1936 to return to his law practice.[39] Another Democrat, Grendel F. Bennett of Marshall, the

[25] *Danville Commercial-News*, November 7, 1930, 1.
[26] *Danville Commercial-News*, November 12, 1930, 1.
[27] *Danville Commercial-News*, December 15, 1930, 1.
[28] State of Illinois Secretary of State, *Abstract of Election Returns 1882-1912*, 319, 355; *Abstract of Votes for County Officers Cast in the County of Vermilion and State of Illinois, at the Election Held in said County, on November 3, 1942*.
[29] Twomey, ed., *Vermilion County Bench and Bar: The First One Hundred Fifty Years 1826-1976*, 32.
[30] *Toledo Democrat*, April 16, 1936, 5.
[31] *Toledo Democrat*, April 23, 1936, 1.
[32] *Toledo Democrat*, April 30, 1936, 1.
[33] State of Illinois Secretary of State, *Abstract of Election Returns 1882-1912*, 325.
[34] Ibid., 287, 288, 298.
[35] Ibid., 245, 246, 247, 256.
[36] Edward J. Hughes, ed., *Blue Book of the State of Illinois, 1933-1934* (Springfield: Journal Printing Co., 1933), 755.
[37] Stratton, ed., *Blue Book of the State of Illinois, 1931-1932*, 687.
[38] Van Meter, *The Legal Profession in Coles County*, 2, 3.
[39] Jack E. Horsley, *History of Craig & Craig, Attorneys 1868-1988* (Ann Arbor: Braun-Brumfield, Inc., 1991), 90.

brother of future Clark County Resident Circuit Judge Caslon K. Bennett,[40] completed the term, after winning a special election on November 3, 1936.[41] He had been an unsuccessful candidate in 1933[42] and lost his reelection bid in 1939.[43]

Platt was reelected in 1939, the last year in which a Democratic candidate won a contested circuit-wide judicial race in the Fifth Circuit, and again in 1945.[44] He resigned on November 1, 1949, when he became a judge of the United States District Court,[45] replacing Danville's Walter C. Lindley, who had been elevated to the United States Court of Appeals.[46] Platt died in 1965 and was succeeded by Henry S. Wise of Danville,[47] who had unsuccessfully run for circuit judge in 1951.[48] George W. Bristow of Paris was the one Republican reelected in 1933.[49] Like Platt, he was again reelected in 1939 and 1945. Bristow served with the Appellate Court of Illinois[50] and was later elected to the Supreme Court,[51] succeeding Danville's Walter T. Gunn.[52]

On January 21, 1936, Jacob Berkowitz was elected city judge of Mattoon, [53] after having been defeated in the Democratic primary election for Coles County judge in 1934.[54] Berkowitz was the last Democrat to be elected city, county, or resident circuit judge in Coles County and served until December 5, 1976, longer than any other judge in the history of the Fifth Circuit. Berkowitz, who also held court in Cook County, was blind.[55] His record of longevity was most closely matched by William J. Sunderman, an unsuccessful candidate for Coles County state's attorney in 1944,[56] who was elected county judge on November 7, 1950[57] and held judicial office until his death on April 19, 1989.[58]

---

[40] The Clark County Democrat, *History of Marshall Illinois and Eastern Clark County* (Marshall: The Clark County Democrat, 1978), 105.

[41] *State of Illinois Official Vote Cast at the General Election 1936*, 52.

[42] Hughes, ed., *Blue Book of the State of Illinois, 1933-1934*, 755.

[43] *State of Illinois Official Vote Cast at the General Election 1940*, 54.

[44] Ibid.; *State of Illinois Official Vote Cast at the General Election 1946*, 34.

[45] *Danville Commercial-News*, November 2, 1949, 1.

[46] Twomey, ed., *Vermilion County Bench and Bar: The First One Hundred Fifty Years 1826-1976*, 23, 24.

[47] Ibid., 25.

[48] *State of Illinois Official Vote Cast at the General Election 1952*, 58.

[49] Hughes, ed., *Blue Book of the State of Illinois, 1933-1934*, 755.

[50] Edward J. Barrett, ed., *Blue Book of the State of Illinois, 1951-1952* (Springfield: State of Illinois Secretary of State, 1952), 110.

[51] *State of Illinois Official Vote Cast at the General Election 1952*, 56; *State of Illinois Official Vote Cast at the General Election 1960*, 59.

[52] Twomey, ed., *Vermilion County Bench and Bar: The First One Hundred Fifty Years 1826-1976*, 27.

[53] *The Daily Journal-Gazette*, January 22, 1936, 1.

[54] *Canvass by Voting Precincts of the Votes Cast at the Primary Election Held in the County of Coles and State of Illinois on Tuesday, April 10, 1934.*

[55] *Mattoon Journal Gazette*, December 4, 1976, 1.

[56] *Canvass by Voting Precincts of the Votes Cast at the General Election Held in the County of Coles and State of Illinois on Tuesday, November 7, 1944.*

[57] *Canvass by Voting Precincts of the Votes Cast at the General Election Held in the County of Coles and State of Illinois on Tuesday, November 7, 1950.*

[58] *Times-Courier*, April 20, 1989, 6.

The Mattoon city election of January 20, 1942, in which Berkowitz was reelected, marked the first nonpartisan election for city judges in Coles County.[59] Charleston followed suit in its city election of September 7, 1948.[60] Meanwhile, in Cumberland County, Millard C. Everhart, who had previously served by appointment as county judge from 1917 to 1918, defeated three-term incumbent County Judge Charles M. Connor in the Republican primary election of April 14, 1942.[61] Everhart held the position of Cumberland County judge for three terms himself, until his defeat on November 2, 1954 to William J. Hill, the last non-attorney to hold office as a judge in the Fifth Circuit.[62] Everhart's grandson, Millard S. Everhart, later served fifteen years as Cumberland County state's attorney and became resident circuit judge on November 26, 2002. Another significant event in the 1940's was the election of Howard T. Ruff to the office of Edgar County judge on November 5, 1946.[63] Ruff held that position until his death on May 27, 1972, longer than any other county, associate, or resident circuit judge in Edgar County history.

On May 25, 1960, the City of Charleston passed an ordinance discontinuing the office of city judge, effective September 6, citing a lack of activity during the previous two years.[64] Coles County State's Attorney Thomas M. Burke, who had unsuccessfully sought the city judge position in 1954,[65] and Jack H. Anderson were candidates for the office and brought mandamus proceedings in the Circuit Court, asking that the 1960 judicial election be held.[66] They were successful, and a primary election took place on July 19, 1960. Anderson and Jack Austin advanced to the general election with vote totals of 687 and 506. Burke garnered only 311 votes, while Alton B. Cofer received 238.[67] Anderson defeated Austin on September 6, 1960[68] and was Charleston's last city judge. He resigned in December, 1962, after passage of an amendment to the constitution, prohibiting judges from engaging in the practice of law.[69] On April 9, 1963, Charleston voters, by a vote of 827 to 380, chose to abolish the office.[70]

By 1962, the Illinois court system had become quite complicated, with many of the courts having overlapping jurisdictions and lacking administrative supervision. As a result, on November 6, 1962, Illinois voters approved an amendment to the constitution, effective January 1, 1964, which revamped the article on the judiciary and established a unified court

---

[59] *Daily Journal-Gazette*, January 20, 1942, 1.

[60] *The Charleston Daily Courier*, September 8, 1948, 1.

[61] *Toledo Democrat*, April 16, 1942, 2.

[62] *Abstract of Votes for County Officers Cast in the County of Cumberland and State of Illinois, at the Election Held in said County, on November 2, 1954.*

[63] *Canvass by Voting Precincts of the Votes Cast at the General Election Held in the County of Edgar and State of Illinois on Tuesday, November 5, 1946.*

[64] *The Charleston Daily Courier*, May 26, 1960, 1.

[65] *The Charleston Daily Courier*, September 8, 1954, 1.

[66] *The Charleston Courier-News*, June 2, 1960, 1.

[67] *The Charleston Courier-News*, July 20, 1960, 1.

[68] *The Charleston Courier-News*, September 7, 1960, 1.

[69] *The Charleston Courier-News*, December 16, 1962, 3; Ill. Const. of 1870 art. VI, sec. 16, as amended in 1962.

[70] *The Charleston Courier-News*, April 10, 1963, 1.

system in Illinois. By virtue of the amendment, the Appellate Court was reorganized, and its judges were to be elected. The Circuit Court assumed unlimited original jurisdiction of all justiciable matters, effectively eliminating the inferior courts. The new article required all judges to be licensed attorneys of the State of Illinois, but prevented them from practicing law. The three circuit judges, Robert F. Cotton of Paris, John F. Spivey of Danville, and Harry I. Hannah of Mattoon, remained as such, while the county, probate, and city judges became associate judges of the Circuit Court. The police magistrates and justices of the peace became magistrates of the Circuit Court.[71]

The amendment to the constitution also provided that the circuit and associate judges in office on January 1, 1963 would not have to run for reelection. Instead, they would be allowed to seek retention by the electorate and hold office for terms of six years, with the circuit judges first standing for retention in 1964 and the associate judges doing so in 1966. The magistrates were to be appointed by the circuit judges without any definite terms. To remain in office, the circuit and associate judges were required to receive the affirmative vote of a majority of the voters of their circuit or county.[72] The highest retention percentages in the history of the Fifth Circuit occurred in the 1960's. Cotton's percentage of affirmative votes in the circuit was 87.05 on November 3, 1964, followed by Spivey's percentage of 86.50 and Hannah's figure of 86.45.[73] William J. Sunderman's percentage of affirmative votes in Coles County was 87.06 on November 8, 1966. Zollie O. Arbogast's percentage in Clark County was 68.30.[74] That is the only time in which a retention percentage of a Fifth Circuit judge has fallen below seventy percent.

The changes brought about by the amendment were refined with the adoption of a new constitution in 1970, which became effective on July 1, 1971. On that date, the associate judges became circuit judges, with terms of six years, and the magistrates became associate judges, still appointed by the circuit judges, with terms of four years. The circuit judges were permitted to seek retention, but required to receive the affirmative vote of three-fifths of the voters of the entire circuit.[75] Spivey and Cotton soon retired, after each serving as a circuit judge for twenty years. Spivey, who had also spent time with the Appellate Court prior to its reorganization,[76] left office on October 1, 1971 to be replaced on October 15, 1971 by former Vermilion County Judge Frank J. Meyer. Cotton departed on December 30, 1971 and was replaced on January 1, 1972 by former Edgar County State's Attorney Ralph S. Pearman. Meyer served through December 14, 1979, when poor health forced him to

---

[71] Rolewick, *A Short History of the Illinois Judicial Systems*, 19, 21, 23, 24; Ill. Const. of 1870 art. VI, preamble, secs. 6, 9, 10, 15, 16, paras. 1, 4, 5, as amended in 1962.

[72] Rolewick, *A Short History of the Illinois Judicial Systems*, 23; Ill. Const. of 1870 art. VI, secs. 11, 12, 14, para. 12, as amended in 1962.

[73] *State of Illinois Official Vote Cast at the General Election 1964*, 140.

[74] *State of Illinois Official Vote Cast at the General Election 1966*, 54-56.

[75] Rolewick, *A Short History of the Illinois Judicial Systems*, 30; Ill. Const. of 1970 preamble, art. VI, secs. 10, 12(d), Transition Schedule sec. 4.

[76] William H. Chamberlain, ed., *Blue Book of the State of Illinois, 1963-1964* (Springfield: State of Illinois Secretary of State, 1964), 114, 146.

retire.[77] He died on December 24, 1979.[78] Pearman remained on the circuit bench through December 6, 1998, longer than any other circuit judge elected at large from the five counties of the Fifth Circuit.

On November 3, 1970, John W. Unger was elected Vermilion County state's attorney. He had been appointed to the office in 1969, after the resignation of John Morton Jones.[79] Unger had been probate judge from 1954 to 1958, when he lost the Republican primary election to future Magistrate Lawrence T. Allen, Jr.,[80] the brother of former State's Attorney John T. Allen and son of a former county judge.[81] Unger died three days after the election.[82] Everett L. Laury completed the term by appointment.[83]

Shortly after Unger's death, other officials of the Fifth Circuit passed away prior to the completion of their terms, including Associate Judge Henri I. Ripstra on December 29, 1971, Edgar County Resident Circuit Judge Ruff on May 27, 1972, Circuit Judge Hannah on May 20, 1973, and Coles County State's Attorney John J. McCarthy on November 29, 1973. Those losses resulted in the appointments of Richard E. Scott on April 1, 1972, Carl A. Lund on October 15, 1972, Thomas M. Burke on October 1, 1973, and Bobby F. Sanders on December 11, 1973.[84] Scott enjoyed a career of thirty-one years as an associate and circuit judge. Former State's Attorney Burke had served as a police magistrate for the City of Charleston, a magistrate for the Fifth Circuit, and an associate judge, before becoming a circuit judge elected at large and, from February 15 to December 2, 1990, a recalled circuit judge assigned to Cumberland County. Sanders lost a special election on November 5, 1974 to Paul C. Komada, who later held office as a circuit judge from 1980 to 2001.

Lund was the resident circuit judge of Edgar County until 1986, when he became the first judge from the Fifth Circuit to be elected to the Appellate Court. He joined Coles County Resident Circuit Judge Joseph R. Spitz, a former justice of the peace, who served with the Appellate Court by assignment from October 21, 1985 until his retirement on October 1, 1991. Vermilion County Resident Circuit Judge Paul M. Wright attempted to serve, but lost the March 19, 1974 primary election,[85] as well as the November 2, 1976 general election.[86] Lund also lost his first primary election for the Appellate Court on March 20, 1984,[87] but won the office on November 4, 1986.[88]

---

[77] *The Commercial-News*, December 19, 1979, 20.

[78] *The Commercial-News*, December 24, 1979, 1.

[79] *The Commercial-News*, November 4, 1970, 17.

[80] *Abstract of Votes for County Officers Cast in the County of Vermilion and State of Illinois, at the Election Held in said County, on November 2, 1954; Danville Commercial-News*, April 10, 1958, 21.

[81] Twomey, ed., *Vermilion County Bench and Bar: The First One Hundred Fifty Years 1826-1976*, 30.

[82] *The Commercial-News*, November 7, 1970, 3.

[83] *The Commercial-News*, November 12, 1970, 23.

[84] *Times-Courier*, December 12, 1973, 1.

[85] *State of Illinois Official Vote Cast at the General Primary Election 1974*, 41.

[86] *State of Illinois Official Vote Cast at the General Election 1976*, 124.

[87] *State of Illinois Official Vote Cast at the General Primary Election 1984*, 152.

[88] *State of Illinois Official Vote Cast at the General Election 1986*, 103.

Rita B. Garman followed Lund on the Appellate Court. Garman became the first female judge of the Fifth Circuit when appointed associate judge on January 7, 1974. On November 4, 1986, she was elected at large to the office of circuit judge.[89] On July 17, 1995, after Lund's retirement, Garman was assigned to the Appellate Court and elected on November 5, 1996.[90] On February 1, 2001, Garman was appointed to the Supreme Court of Illinois, to which she was elected on November 5, 2002.[91]

As an associate and circuit judge, Garman worked in Vermilion County with Circuit Judges Frank J. Meyer and John P. Meyer, who were brothers;[92] Matthew A. Jurczak, a retired associate judge who was appointed circuit judge upon John P. Meyer's retirement; Paul M. Wright; and James K. Robinson. Wright, a Democrat, had initially been elected probate judge in 1958.[93] Robinson, a Republican, had initially been elected county judge in 1962.[94] The two did not get along, but served together for a longer period than that served by any other judge in Vermilion County, and both retired on the same day: August 1, 1987. Robinson was brought out of retirement on January 15, 1990 and assigned to Clark County, after the death of Resident Circuit Judge Arbogast on November 28, 1989.

On April 19, 1981, Tracy W. Resch, a Democrat, resigned the office of Clark County state's attorney to return to private practice.[95] On April 24, 1981, David W. Lewis was appointed to the position, despite having voted Republican in the most recent primary election. The Clark County Democratic Central Committee took exception to the appointment of Lewis, believing it to be contrary to state law. After unsuccessfully seeking action from the Attorney General and from State's Attorney Lewis himself,[96] the chairman of the Committee filed a quo warranto lawsuit in Clark County,[97] which was ultimately dismissed by Circuit Judge Wright, who ruled that the chairman lacked sufficient interest to bring the suit.[98] Lewis was elected to the office as a Republican on November 2, 1982[99] and served longer than any other Clark County state's attorney. He resigned on October 15, 2001 to fill an associate judge vacancy. Resch was elected resident circuit judge of Clark County on November 6, 1990,[100] and has held that office longer than any other judge in Clark County.

---

[89] Ibid., 111.

[90] *State of Illinois Official Vote Cast at the General Election 1996*, 100.

[91] "Rita B. Garman, Supreme Court Justice Fourth District," Welcome to Illinois Courts. State of Illinois, http://state.il.us/court/SupremeCourt/Justices/Bio_Garman.asp.

[92] *The Commercial-News*, December 19, 1979, 20.

[93] *Abstract of Votes for County Officers Cast in the County of Vermilion and State of Illinois, at the Election Held in said County, on November 4, 1958.*

[94] *Danville Commercial-News*, November 11, 1962, 21.

[95] *Marshall Independent*, April 13, 1981, 1.

[96] *Marshall Independent*, May 7, 1981, 1.

[97] *Marshall Independent*, May 11, 1981, 1.

[98] *Marshall Independent*, July 13, 1981, 1.

[99] *Marshall Independent*, November 4, 1982, 1.

[100] *State of Illinois Official Vote Cast at the General Election 1990*, 118-119.

The Fifth Circuit lost three of its circuit judges in 1989. William J. Sunderman of Coles County died on April 19, shortly after announcing that he would retire on May 1.[101] On December 9, eleven days after the passing of Arbogast, James R. Watson died. Elected in 1966, Watson was Cumberland County's longest tenured judge. By necessity, retired Circuit Judges Robinson and Burke were recalled to the bench. In the election of November 6, 1990, former Cumberland County State's Attorney Robert B. Cochonour was elected resident circuit judge of Cumberland County.[102] Cochonour was popular among the lawyers and citizens of the circuit. However, he resigned on May 7, 2002, amid reports of improprieties in his handling, as executor, of a wealthy estate. On January 3, 2003, Cochonour pled guilty to a charge of "Theft of Property Exceeding $100,000" and was sentenced to seven years in prison.[103]

On August 20, 1995, the General Assembly added a fourth circuit judge, elected at large, to the Fifth Circuit.[104] Dale A. Cini of Mattoon, who had been an associate judge assigned to Coles County since February 1, 1993, was elected to that position, after defeating candidates from Vermilion County in both the primary and general elections of 1996.[105] As a result, for the first time in eighty-one years, a county of the Fifth Circuit claimed more than one judge elected circuit-wide, as Cini joined Paul C. Komada from Coles County. Upon Cini's retirement on January 7, 2008, retired Circuit Judge Richard E. Scott was recalled, effective March 3, 2008, to complete the term. When Scott himself retired on July 8, 2010, Edgar County State's Attorney Matthew L. Sullivan, the unopposed Republican candidate for the vacancy in the November 2, 2010 election, was appointed, effective July 9, 2010. Sullivan's service of nearly fourteen years as state's attorney was longer than that of any other elected prosecutor in Edgar County.

The election of a non-Vermilion County resident to the newly-created circuit opening inspired additional legislation on November 11, 1997, which created a third resident circuit judge position in Vermilion County.[106] State's Attorney Michael D. Clary edged Charles C. Hall by thirteen votes in the election for that position on November 3, 1998, a vote which also featured the election of Danville's Claudia S. Anderson to the circuit-wide vacancy created by Garman's move to the Appellate Court and Mattoon's James R. Glenn to another circuit-wide vacancy resulting from Pearman's retirement.[107] From then until the retirement of Cini, Coles County residents filled three of the four at large circuit judge slots. Mitchell K. Shick of Charleston succeeded Komada as one of the circuit judges elected at large. He defeated Coles County State's Attorney C. Steve Ferguson, the longest serving state's attorney

[101] *Times-Courier*, April 20, 1989, 1, 6.
[102] *State of Illinois Official Vote Cast at the General Election 1990*, 118-119.
[103] *Charleston Times-Courier*, January 4, 2003, 1.
[104] 705 ILCS 35/2h(b) (2008).
[105] *State of Illinois Official Vote Cast at the General Primary Election 1996*, 197; *State of Illinois Official Vote Cast at the General Election 1996*, 122.
[106] 705 ILCS 35/2j(d) (2008).
[107] *State of Illinois Official Vote Cast at the General Election 1998*, 126-127.

in the history of Coles County, in the November 5, 2002 election.[108] Clary and Anderson served in Vermilion County with former State's Attorney and Resident Circuit Judge Thomas J. Fahey and later worked with Fahey's wife, Nancy S. Fahey, who was elected on November 7, 2006 to the vacancy created by her husband's retirement.[109]

---

[108] *State of Illinois Official Vote Cast at the General Election 2002*, 145.
[109] *State of Illinois Official Vote Cast at the General Election 2006*, 136.

III

ASSOCIATE JUDGES

The amended judicial article of the Illinois Constitution of 1870, which took effect on January 1, 1964, created the position of magistrate and abolished the justice of the peace and police magistrate courts. The circuit judges were authorized to appoint magistrates to serve at their pleasure, without terms. The justices of the peace and police magistrates then in office became magistrates of the Circuit Court and were permitted to complete their terms, while performing non-judicial functions.[1]

Shortly before the amendment took effect, the following persons held office in the Fifth Circuit as justices of the peace:

Clark County: Charles W. Savage of Casey, B. Otto Ray of Marshall, and Robert A. Weaver of Marshall;

Coles County: Russell W. Towles of Charleston and Joseph R. Spitz of Mattoon;

Cumberland County: Rufus Carrell of Greenup, Walter H. Bingaman of Neoga, and Joseph Zike of Toledo;

Edgar County: Bert H. Ellsberry of Chrisman, David O. Kime of Kansas, and Charles E. Shaw of Paris; and

Vermilion County: Robert B. Kerby of Danville, Bernard E. Schackmann of Danville, William E. Wayland of Danville, Orrin J. Gray of Rossville, and Austin Stark of Westville.

The following persons served the circuit as police magistrates:

Coles County: Thomas M. Burke of Charleston, Frank French of Mattoon, and Lee Roy Andrews of Oakland;

Cumberland County: Arthur V. McElravy of Greenup; and

---

[1] Rolewick, *A Short History of the Illinois Judicial Systems*, 19, 23; Ill. Const. of 1870 art. VI, preamble, secs. 8, 12, paras. 1, 4(e), 5(a), as amended in 1962.

<u>Vermilion County</u>: Clarence C. Brown of Allerton, Fred W. Prettyman of Danville, Clarence Wisecup of Fithian, Elza B. Pearson of Georgetown, Ruth E. Crose of Hoopeston, Harry Christansen of Rankin, Vera M. Lyons of Tilton, and Peter P. Godels of Westville.

All of those individuals became magistrates on January 1, 1964.

On March 22, 1965, the chief judge of the Fifth Circuit, Robert F. Cotton, entered an administrative order, terminating the duties of most of the magistrates as of April 1, 1965. Prettyman, whose term did not expire until 1967, remained. The Fifth Circuit, based on its population and number of associate judges, was authorized to select a total of four magistrates.[2] Accordingly, the following were appointed, with their service to begin on April 1, 1965: Matthew A. Jurczak and John F. Twomey, who were assigned to Vermilion County; Mark B. Hunt, who was assigned to Coles County; and Henri I. Ripstra, who was assigned to Clark, Cumberland, and Edgar Counties. Ripstra had been an unsuccessful candidate for Clark County state's attorney in the Republican primary election of April 8, 1952.[3]

Hunt resigned and was replaced by former Police Magistrate Burke on August 1, 1966. Prettyman's term expired on April 4, 1967. Afterwards, Chief Judge John F. Spivey successfully obtained approval from the Supreme Court for the appointment of an additional magistrate, which was utilized by necessity in Vermilion County. Lawrence T. Allen, Jr. was appointed over three other applicants, effective December 15, 1967.

On July 1, 1971, the most recent constitution of the State of Illinois took effect. It provided that the associate judges of the Circuit Court would become circuit judges and the magistrates would become associate judges.[4] At the direction of the Supreme Court, the circuit judges of the Fifth Circuit reappraised the qualifications of the five magistrates. After a poll of the attorneys, magistrates, and judges of the circuit established that eighty percent of those voting favored retention, the circuit judges unanimously approved retention of Magistrates Jurczak, Twomey, Ripstra, Burke, and Allen as associate judges under the new constitution. When Ripstra died on December 29, 1971, Richard E. Scott was appointed to fill the vacancy, effective April 1, 1972. Scott was selected from a pool of six candidates, one of whom was future Cumberland County State's Attorney and Circuit Judge Robert B. Cochonour.

On October 1, 1973, Burke was appointed circuit judge to fill the vacancy created by the death of Harry I. Hannah. That left an associate judge vacancy, which was filled by Tom E. Grace on February 1, 1974. Grace was selected from a group of ten candidates, which included future Coles County State's Attorney and Circuit Judge Paul C. Komada, former Coles County State's Attorney L. Stanton Dotson, and future Vermilion County State's Attorney Edward Litak. Meanwhile, Twomey retired on January 1, 1974 and was replaced by Rita B. Garman on January 7, 1974. Garman, the first female judge of the Fifth Circuit, was selected from that same group of ten candidates.

---

[2] 1963 Ill. Laws 2645.

[3] *Clark County Democrat*, April 10, 1952, 1.

[4] Ill. Const. of 1970 preamble, art. VI, Transition Schedule sec. 4.

In 1975 and 1979, Associate Judges Jurczak, Allen, Scott, Garman, and Grace were reappointed by the circuit judges for terms of four years. The Supreme Court provided that the terms of all associate judges in office on June 30, 1975 would expire on that date and on every fourth anniversary of that date, regardless of when first appointed.[5]

Grace retired on May 1, 1980. In an election involving ten candidates, including future Judge Ashton C. Waller, future Coles County State's Attorney Nancy W. Owen, and Dotson, Loren J. Kabbes was appointed to fill the vacancy on that date. The service of Kabbes was brief. On May 4, 1982, he was arrested for "Driving Under the Influence of Alcohol." Kabbes resigned his position, effective June 30, 1983, and was not reappointed by the circuit judges in the 1983 balloting.

Prior to that balloting, a judicial advisory poll was taken by the Illinois State Bar Association for the retention of the associate judges. Scott and Garman scored well. On April 12, 1983, Jurczak and Allen each submitted their resignations. Jurczak's retirement would be effective as of July 2, 1984. Allen's would take effect on July 5, 1984. Both were reappointed by the circuit judges, subject to their departures in 1984. Allen attempted to withdraw his resignation on March 15, 1984, but it was considered irrevocable, and his term did expire. Jurczak was appointed circuit judge in 1986.

Waller was appointed to fill the Kabbes vacancy, effective July 1, 1983. He was selected from a pool of twelve candidates, which included former Coles County State's Attorneys Dotson and Bobby F. Sanders, as well as William A. Sunderman, the son of Circuit Judge William J. Sunderman. Later, Joseph C. Moore and Joseph P. Skowronski were appointed to fill the Jurczak and Allen slots, beginning July 6, 1984. They were among twenty-one applicants, two of whom were future Judges David G. Bernthal and Thomas J. Fahey. Fahey had previously served as Vermilion County state's attorney.

The other two associate judges, Scott and Garman, both of whom had been reappointed in 1983, became circuit judges in 1986. Garman was elected to the office and resigned her associate judgeship on December 1, 1986. Fourteen attorneys applied to fill her vacancy, including future Judges James K. Borbely, Claudia S. Anderson, Michael D. Clary, and Craig H. DeArmond. DeArmond was the Vermilion County state's attorney at that time. Clary would succeed him. Bernthal received the appointment, effective January 1, 1987. Scott was appointed circuit judge and resigned his associate judgeship on December 3, 1986. Ten attorneys applied to fill his vacancy, including Clark County State's Attorney and future Associate Judge David W. Lewis, future Circuit Judge Steven L. Garst, and former Edgar County State's Attorney Arthur A. Jones. H. Dean Andrews received the appointment, which took effect on February 1, 1987. Waller, Moore, Skowronski, Bernthal, and Andrews were all reappointed to their positions in 1987.

Waller became a circuit judge and resigned his associate judge position on June 1, 1989. In an election involving six candidates, one of whom was Coles County State's Attorney Owen, Gary W. Jacobs was appointed by the circuit judges to fill the vacancy. He took office

---

[5] Ill. Sup. Ct. R. 39(a)(1).

on August 1, 1989. Jacobs was reappointed, along with Moore, Skowronski, Bernthal, and Andrews, for a four-year term, beginning July 1, 1991. However, on September 3, 1991, Moore resigned. In an election involving eighteen candidates, including Clary, DeArmond, and future Vermilion County State's Attorney Larry S. Mills, Borbely was appointed to the position. He took office on September 4, 1991.

Jacobs and Bernthal each vacated their offices prior to the next retention balloting. Jacobs was elected circuit judge and therefore resigned his position on December 7, 1992. Thirteen persons applied to fill his vacancy, including Dotson, Lewis, and future Circuit Judges James R. Glenn and Mitchell K. Shick. Dale A. Cini received the appointment, effective February 1, 1993. Bernthal was selected United States magistrate judge and resigned his position on April 30, 1995. In an election involving twenty-two candidates, including future Circuit Judges Clary and Nancy S. Fahey, future Vermilion County State's Attorneys Frank R. Young and Randall J. Brinegar, and former Edgar County State's Attorney Michael M. McFatridge, Gordon R. Stipp was appointed to fill the vacancy. He took office on May 15, 1995. Cini and Stipp, along with Skowronski, Andrews, and Borbely, were reappointed for four-year terms, beginning July 1, 1995.

On July 17, 1995, Circuit Judge Garman was assigned to the Appellate Court. To help ease the burden on the Vermilion County court system, retired Associate Judge Moore was recalled as an associate judge on September 25, 1995 to serve until December 2, 1996. His term was later extended to February 28, 1997, at which time he again retired. The vacancy in the Circuit Court was filled on April 21, 1997 by the appointment of Claudia S. Anderson.

After the legislature increased the number of at large circuit judges in the Fifth Circuit from three to four,[6] Cini was elected to the newly-created position, and resigned his associate judgeship on December 2, 1996. Fifteen attorneys applied to fill his vacancy, including Lewis and Glenn. Teresa K. Righter received the appointment, effective January 13, 1997. Afterwards, in the 1999 retention balloting, the circuit judges reappointed Skowronski, Andrews, Borbely, Stipp, and Righter for subsequent terms.

On November 11, 1997, the General Assembly added a resident circuit judge position in Vermilion County,[7] which was filled on December 7, 1998. That action inadvertently resulted in the loss of an associate judge slot, as the circuit had three resident circuit judge positions in excess of one per county and, due to the circuit's population, an allowable number of population-based associate judgeships of three. It did still have the permissive associate judgeship approved by the Supreme Court in 1967. When Andrews was elected circuit judge and resigned his associate judge position on December 4, 2000, the Administrative Office of the Illinois Courts denied authorization to fill the vacancy.

The legislature resolved the issue by amending the Associate Judges Act on June 28, 2001. The Fifth Circuit, with a population in excess of 173,000, became entitled to a minimum

---

[6] 705 ILCS 35/2h(b) (2008).
[7] 705 ILCS 35/2j(d) (2008).

number of five associate judges.[8] An election resulted, involving twenty-two candidates, which included future Judges Garst and Brien J. O'Brien, Edgar County State's Attorney and future Circuit Judge Matthew L. Sullivan, former Edgar County State's Attorney McFatridge, and future Clark County State's Attorney Dennis E. Simonton. David W. Lewis was appointed to fill the Andrews vacancy and took office on October 15, 2001. After the amended legislation passed, the director of the Administrative Office advised that the Fifth Circuit still retained the permissive associate judgeship, in addition to the five population-based associate judge positions provided by statute. The State of Illinois was facing a financial crisis at that time, however, and the circuit judges chose to temporarily hold the number of associate judgeships at five.

Righter, who was reappointed in 2003 with Skowronski, Borbely, Stipp, and Lewis, resigned her associate judge position on December 6, 2004, when she became a circuit judge. The ensuing election involved twenty-three candidates, including State's Attorneys Sullivan, Simonton, and Barry E. Schaefer, the latter serving in Cumberland County. O'Brien was appointed by the circuit judges to the office and assumed his duties on February 22, 2005. He was reappointed, along with Skowronski, Borbely, Stipp, and Lewis, in 2007.

Vermilion County endured three associate judge vacancies within a period of nine months. Borbely retired on November 1, 2009. Twenty applicants sought to fill his vacancy, including future Associate Judge Derek J. Girton, an unsuccessful candidate for Vermilion County state's attorney in the February 5, 2008 Democratic primary election. Mark S. Goodwin was appointed, effective December 4, 2009. Then, on August 1, 2010, Skowronski and Stipp both retired. Skowronski's service of twenty-six years was longer than that of any other magistrate or associate judge of the Fifth Circuit. In an election involving twenty-two candidates, Girton and Karen E. Wall were appointed to fill the vacancies. They took office on August 9, 2010.

---

[8] 705 ILCS 45/2(a) (2008).

IV

ADMINISTRATION

As Illinois grew and its court system expanded during its first 144 years of existence, great organizational problems emerged. Illinois courts were plentiful, with overlapping jurisdictions, and lacked an administrative authority to unify, coordinate, and supervise them. The amended judicial article of the Illinois Constitution of 1870, effective January 1, 1964, responded to those difficulties by establishing a unified court system. In addition to vesting general administrative authority over all Illinois courts in the Supreme Court, to be exercised by its chief justice, the new article gave general administrative authority in each circuit to a chief judge, who was also authorized to provide for various divisions within the circuit. The chief judge would be a circuit judge, selected by the circuit and associate judges to serve at their pleasure.[1]

The circuit judges of the Fifth Circuit at the time of the amendment were Robert F. Cotton of Paris, John F. Spivey of Danville, and Harry I. Hannah of Mattoon. On January 2, 1964, after months of planning, the circuit and associate judges entered an administrative order, which named Cotton as the circuit's first chief judge. Cotton's term commenced on January 1, 1964. The judges then provided that each of the five counties of the circuit would have a general division, a county division, and a magistrate division. Vermilion County would also have a probate division. The judges also adopted Rules of Practice and Rules of Court, which provided that in November of each even-numbered year, the circuit and associate judges would meet to vote on whether the chief judge then in office should be retained for the next two years. The chief judge would designate a presiding judge for each division of the court, who would serve at the pleasure of the chief judge. The duty of the presiding judge was to supervise all of the judicial activities of the division over which he or she presided.

Hannah and Cotton were designated the presiding judges of the five general divisions of the circuit in alternative rotations of four months. Spivey also served. The first presiding

---

[1] Rolewick, *A Short History of the Illinois Judicial Systems*, 19, 21, 23; Ill. Const. of 1870 art. VI, preamble, secs. 2, 8, para. 1, as amended in 1962.

judges of both the county and magistrate divisions in each county of the circuit were as follows: Zollie O. Arbogast in Clark County, William J. Sunderman in Coles County, William J. Hill in Cumberland County, and Howard T. Ruff in Edgar County. Hill retired in 1966 and Arbogast resigned in 1967. James K. Robinson was named presiding judge in the county division of Vermilion County, while Paul M. Wright attained the position in both the probate and magistrate divisions.

Cotton was retained as chief judge in November, 1964, but resigned at the conclusion of his term in 1966. His secretary was Mildred P. Weston. On December 5, 1966, Spivey became the circuit's second chief judge. His secretary was Mildred J. Towle, who assumed the title of administrative secretary on July 26, 1967.[2] Spivey served only one term under an agreement that the office of chief judge would rotate among the circuit judges every two years. On December 2, 1968, Hannah became the circuit's third chief judge. Sibyl E. Etchason served as his administrative secretary. The next retention vote for the chief judge position was scheduled for December 18, 1970, but postponed to February 15, 1971. At that meeting, Hannah was retained as chief judge for another term of two years, which would expire in January, 1973. However, he resigned the position as of February 1, 1972.

On July 1, 1971, the most recent constitution of the State of Illinois took effect. It provided that the associate judges would become circuit judges and the magistrates would become associate judges. It also required the circuit judges to select a chief judge from their number to serve at their pleasure. The chief judge continued to have general administrative authority over the court, including the authority to provide for various divisions.[3] In response, Hannah entered an administrative order, changing the designation of the magistrate division to the primary division.

On August 10, 1971, Caslon K. Bennett became the presiding judge of the general and county divisions of Clark County and James R. Watson became the presiding judge of those divisions in Cumberland County. In Coles County, Hannah became the presiding judge of the general division, while Sunderman remained in charge of the county division. In Edgar County, Cotton became the presiding judge of the general division, while Ruff remained responsible for the county division. In Vermilion County, the presiding judges were as follows: general division-Spivey, county division-Robinson, probate division-Wright, and primary division-Associate Judge John F. Twomey. Spivey retired later that year, leading to the appointment of Wright as the presiding judge of the county's general division on October 5, 1971. Frank J. Meyer succeeded Wright as the presiding judge of the probate division on January 24, 1972, the same date on which Ruff succeeded Cotton, who also retired, as the presiding judge of Edgar County's general division and Ralph S. Pearman became the presiding judge of its county division. Ruff died on May 27, 1972.

Jacob Berkowitz of Mattoon was elected on January 14, 1972 to serve as the circuit's fourth chief judge. His term was to be from February 1, 1972 through July 1, 1973. Prior to the vote, it was moved and seconded that each of the nine existing circuit judges who had

---

[2] 1967 Ill. Laws 2042.

[3] Ill. Const. of 1970 preamble, art. VI, sec. 7(c), Transition Schedule sec. 4.

not served as chief judge serve as such for a period of one year each in the order of seniority, based upon length of judicial service. Many objections were raised to the motion, which was abandoned after lengthy discussion. Berkowitz was the senior judge of the circuit, having first been elected judge of the Mattoon City Court in 1936. He was reelected chief judge on June 1, 1973 and June 7, 1974.

On July 25, 1972, Berkowitz reorganized the divisions of the Circuit Court in Vermilion County and eliminated divisions altogether in the other counties. Beginning on September 5, 1972, Vermilion County would have a criminal division, a civil division, and a general division. Robinson was named the first presiding judge of the criminal division, while Meyer presided in the civil division and Wright did so in the general division. The initial terms were for six months, but Robinson, Meyer, and Wright rotated as presiding judges of each division after varying periods of time. The presiding judges of the other counties, effective September 5, 1972, were as follows: Bennett in Clark County, Hannah in Coles County, Watson in Cumberland County, and Pearman in Edgar County. Hannah died on May 20, 1973. On July 13, 1973, Berkowitz named Sunderman presiding judge of Coles County, effective September 4, 1973.

On June 25, 1976, the election of the circuit's fifth chief judge was conducted. The circuit judges in order of seniority at that time were: Berkowitz (1936), Sunderman (1950), Wright (1958), Robinson (1962), Watson (1966), Bennett (1968), Meyer (1971), Pearman (1972), Carl A. Lund of Edgar County (1972), and Thomas M. Burke of Coles County (1973). Instead of selecting a chief judge on the basis of seniority, or having the office based in either Coles or Vermilion Counties, the judges, in a compromise, elected Pearman to the position, beginning September 7, 1976. Pearman's office was in Paris, but his administrative secretary, Sibyl E. Etchason, remained in Charleston until April, 1977. Etchason then joined Pearman in Paris.

On January 4, 1977, Pearman divided the Circuit Court in Coles County into three divisions: criminal, civil, and general. Effective February 1, 1977, Burke became the presiding judge of the criminal division, while Sunderman assumed the position in the county division and Joseph R. Spitz did so in the general division. Those divisions, however, as well as those in Vermilion County, remained in effect only until October 14, 1977, when the Rules of Practice for the Fifth Judicial Circuit of Illinois were adopted. The Rules of Practice provided that the chief judge would designate one circuit judge within each county of the circuit to sit as the presiding judge of that county and that he or she would sit at the pleasure of the chief judge. On October 21, 1977, Pearman designated the following as presiding judges: Clark County-Bennett, Coles County-Sunderman, Cumberland County-Watson, Edgar County-Pearman, and Vermilion County-Meyer.

The Rules of Practice also provided that the term of the chief judge would be two years, beginning on the last Friday of January, 1979. The chief judge was permitted by the Rules to succeed himself in office. Pearman was reelected chief judge on December 28, 1978, January 9, 1981, December 21, 1982, December 14, 1984, December 22, 1986, December 28, 1988, January 4, 1991, and December 11, 1992.

Meyer retired on December 15, 1979. Robinson became the presiding judge of Vermilion County on December 24, 1979 and was succeeded by Wright on January 4, 1985. After Wright announced his retirement, Pearman named Rita B. Garman to the position of presiding judge of Vermilion County, effective July 13, 1987. Paul C. Komada became the presiding judge of Coles County on June 9, 1986. In Clark County, Bennett retired on December 4, 1988 and was succeeded in the resident circuit judge position by his predecessor, Zollie O. Arbogast, who suddenly died on November 28, 1989. In Cumberland County, Watson died on December 9, 1989. As a result, retired Circuit Judges Robinson and Burke were recalled to service, and on January 26, 1990, they were named presiding judges. Robinson served in Clark County and Burke in Cumberland County through December 2, 1990, the day before Tracy W. Resch and Robert B. Cochonour took office after being elected to fill the vacancies.

Sibyl Etchason's title changed from administrative secretary to administrative assistant on October 29, 1985.[4] After serving three chief judges over a period of twenty-three years, Etchason retired as of December 31, 1991. Ann E. Staats of Paris became the administrative assistant on December 16, 1991, working with Etchason for sixteen days.

At the meeting of the circuit judges on December 16, 1994, Pearman announced that he did not wish to seek another term. The judges then selected Richard E. Scott of Paris to be the circuit's sixth chief judge. His term commenced on January 27, 1995, and Scott was reelected on November 15, 1996 and December 22, 1998. The latter election was first scheduled for November 6, 1998, but postponed until December to permit the newly-elected circuit judges to participate. Scott made several appointments. On July 17, 1995, when Garman was assigned to the Appellate Court, Scott appointed John P. O'Rourke to the presiding judge position in Vermilion County. When O'Rourke announced his retirement at the end of his term in 2000, Scott replaced him with Thomas J. Fahey, effective November 3, 2000. On October 30, 1998, Scott changed presiding judges in Coles County, naming Ashton C. Waller. On December 8, 1998, after Pearman's retirement, Scott himself assumed the role of presiding judge of Edgar County.

Scott also announced his retirement in 2000. Although his term expired on December 4 of that year, the meeting to elect the next chief judge was not scheduled until December 18. Scott entered an administrative order, naming James R. Glenn of Mattoon acting chief judge from November 27, 2000 to January 26, 2001, or until such date as a new chief judge is elected. Glenn appointed H. Dean Andrews to the position of presiding judge of Edgar County, effective December 4, 2000. The December 18 meeting was postponed to January 10, 2001 and the election to January 24, 2001.

At the January 24, 2001 meeting of the circuit judges, Waller, a resident of Charleston, was elected chief judge of the Fifth Circuit, beginning his term on January 25, 2001. During that term, on May 7, 2002, Cochonour resigned his circuit judgeship, leading to the appointment of Resch as the presiding judge of Cumberland County, effective May 9, 2002. He was succeeded on November 27, 2002 by Millard S. Everhart, who was appointed

---

[4] 705 ILCS 35/4.1 (2008).

and then elected resident circuit judge of that county. When Waller himself announced his retirement, Gary W. Jacobs was named the presiding judge of Coles County, effective September 8, 2003.

Glenn was elected chief judge at the meeting of December 19, 2002 and reelected on January 11, 2005, beginning his service on January 31, 2003. The latter election had been scheduled for December 9, 2004, but was postponed until an amendment to the Rules of Practice could be considered. The amendment, which required that the selection of the chief judge be made on a nonpartisan basis and prohibited one's service as chief judge for more than two consecutive two-year terms, passed during the January 11, 2005 meeting. Glenn formally appointed Resch, who had been the resident circuit judge of Clark County since December 3, 1990, presiding judge of his home county. Upon Fahey's resignation as Vermilion County's presiding judge, Glenn appointed Claudia S. Anderson to succeed him, effective September 2, 2005. H. Dean Andrews retired from the judiciary on August 1, 2006, leading Glenn to fill in as presiding judge of Edgar County from then until September 8, 2006, when Steven L. Garst took office.

Resch, a Marshall resident, was elected the circuit's ninth chief judge on December 6, 2006 and reelected on December 5, 2008. Beginning his service on January 26, 2007, Resch was the first chief judge to reside outside of Coles, Edgar, or Vermilion Counties. Early in his first term, Resch was confronted with a vacancy in the administrative assistant position, as Ann E. Staats retired on April 30, 2007. Kathy Lay succeeded her on May 2, 2007. Later, Anderson resigned her presiding judge position in Vermilion County, which was filled by Michael D. Clary, effective October 3, 2009. Upon Jacobs' retirement on January 7, 2011, Resch appointed Teresa K. Righter to succeed him as the presiding judge of Coles County.

On December 3, 2010, Everhart, a Toledo resident, was elected the tenth chief judge of the Fifth Circuit, beginning his first term on January 28, 2011. In forty-seven years, each of the counties of the Fifth Judicial Circuit has had a resident serve in the office of chief judge.

ELECTIONS

	Votes	Pct.
FOURTH CIRCUIT		
CIRCUIT JUDGE		
Clark, Coles, and Cumberland		
September 4, 1848		
Justin Harlan	3,031	44
William Wilson	2,062	30
Charles H. Constable	1,859	27
Clark, Coles, Cumberland, and Edgar		
June 4, 1855		
Justin Harlan	9,839	99
Elisha H. Starkweather	75	1
June 3, 1861		
Charles H. Constable	2,527	65
Justin Harlan	1,358	35
Clark and Cumberland		
June 3, 1867		
Hiram B. Decius	3,637	62
Justin Harlan	2,268	38
STATE'S ATTORNEY		
Clark, Coles, and Cumberland		
September 4, 1848		
Alfred Kitchell	5,003	100
November 2, 1852		
Alfred Kitchell	8,668	100
Clark, Coles, Cumberland, and Edgar		
November 4, 1856		
John Scholfield	8,459	57
William W. Craddock	6,276	43
November 6, 1860		
James R. Cunningham	7,028	53
Joseph G. Cannon	6,239	47
November 8, 1864		
Silas S. Whitehead	10,057	57
James A. Connelly	7,310	42
Francis A. Allen	142	1

	Votes	Pct.
Clark and Cumberland		
November 3, 1868		
Silas S. Whitehead	7,510	58
Robert A. Campbell	5,519	42
EIGHTH CIRCUIT		
CIRCUIT JUDGE		
Edgar and Vermilion		
September 4, 1848		
David Davis	7,852	100
Vermilion		
June 4, 1855		
David Davis	14,049	100
STATE'S ATTORNEY		
Edgar and Vermilion		
September 4, 1848		
David B. Campbell	7,719	100
November 2, 1852		
David B. Campbell	10,026	53
A. M. Broadwell	8,744	47
Vermilion		
November 4, 1856		
Ward H. Lamon	10,783	53
Major W. Packard	9,578	47
November 6, 1860		
Ward H. Lamon	11,847	100
TWENTY-SEVENTH CIRCUIT		
CIRCUIT JUDGE		
Vermilion		
June 3, 1861		
Oliver L. Davis	543	100
Coles, Edgar, and Vermilion		
June 3, 1867		
James Steele	4,734	57
James A. Eads	3,548	43
STATE'S ATTORNEY		
Vermilion		
November 8, 1864		
Joseph G. Cannon	5,892	61
Thomas M. Macaughtney	3,807	39

Coles, Edgar, and Vermilion
November 3, 1868

John Boyle	9,529	55
Thomas E. Bundy	7,822	45

FIFTEENTH CIRCUIT
CIRCUIT JUDGE
Clark, Coles, Edgar, and Vermilion
June 2, 1873

Oliver L. Davis	4,965	54
James Steele	3,500	38
John Pearson	718	8

TWENTY-FIRST CIRCUIT
CIRCUIT JUDGE
Cumberland
June 2, 1873

James C. Allen	4,506	55
Hiram B. Decius	3,714	45

SECOND CIRCUIT
CIRCUIT JUDGE
Cumberland
August 6, 1877

John H. Halley	6,971	51
Edward R. Green	6,569	49

June 2, 1879

Chauncey S. Conger	12,642	21
Thomas S. Casey	11,859	20
William C. Jones	11,293	19
Benson Wood	9,595	16
James C. Allen	7,160	12
William G. Bowman	5,487	9
Lloyd Crouch	931	2
William J. Crews	681	1

June 1, 1885

William C. Jones	12,836	32
Chauncey S. Conger	12,803	32
Carroll C. Boggs	12,685	32
Benson Wood	1,040	3
E. B. Green	156	0

June 1, 1891

Carroll C. Boggs	18,060	20
Silas Z. Landes	17,700	20
Edmund D. Youngblood	17,413	19
Benson Wood	12,597	14
George B. Leonard	11,865	13
T. W. Hutchinson	11,676	13
Peter A. Brady	407	0

FOURTH CIRCUIT
CIRCUIT JUDGE
Clark, Coles, Edgar, and Vermilion
August 6, 1877

William E. Nelson	11,408	53
Jacob W. Wilkin	10,015	47

June 2, 1879

Charles B. Smith	13,757	22
Jacob W. Wilkin	13,028	21
Oliver L. Davis	12,290	20
William E. Nelson	10,534	17
Orlando B. Ficklin	9,019	15
A. Browder Burns	2,963	5

June 1, 1885

Jacob W. Wilkin	20,058	24
James F. Hughes	16,116	20
Charles B. Smith	15,539	19
C. A. Ewing	13,984	17
James W. Craig	12,644	15
William R. Griffith	4,057	5

June 4, 1888 - Wilkin Vacancy

Edward P. Vail	12,248	79
David L. Burns	3,168	21

June 1, 1891

Edward P. Vail	19,801	20
Francis M. Wright	19,216	19
Ferdinand Bookwalter	19,017	19
James W. Graham	16,254	16
James F. Hughes	12,801	13
Charles B. Smith	12,337	12

FIFTH CIRCUIT
CIRCUIT JUDGE

June 7, 1897

Henry Van Sellar, R	14,484	18
Frank K. Dunn, R	14,102	18
Ferdinand Bookwalter, R	14,088	18
James W. Craig, D	12,581	16
George Tilton, D	11,765	15
Frederick W. Dundas, D	11,698	15

June 1, 1903

E. R. E. Kimbrough, D	13,865	18
James W. Craig, D	13,430	17
Morton W. Thompson, R	12,858	16
Fenton W. Booth, R	12,847	16
Henry Van Sellar, R	12,777	16
Lyle Decius, D	12,010	15
Francis A. Allison	543	1

June 7, 1909

E. R. E. Kimbrough, D	13,620	20
Morton W. Thompson, R	12,237	18
William B. Scholfield, D	11,500	17
John H. Marshall, R	11,369	17
Isaac A. Love, R	10,153	15
Andrew J. Hunter, D	8,983	13

June 7, 1915

Augustus A. Partlow, R	14,501	20
Walter Brewer, R	13,614	19
John H. Marshall, R	13,196	18
James W. Craig, D	10,899	15
Andrew B. Dennis, D	10,736	15
Walter V. Arbuckle, D	8,794	12

June 6, 1921

Walter Brewer, R	4,814	34
Augustus A. Partlow, R	4,780	33
John H. Marshall, R	4,744	33

June 6, 1927

John H. Marshall, R	19,203	19
George W. Bristow, R	17,474	17
S. Murray Clark, R	17,389	17
W. O. Edwards, D	16,301	16
Paul B. Lauher, D	16,166	16
T. N. Cofer, D	15,796	15

October 18, 1927 - Marshall Vacancy

Charles A. Shuey, R	9,811	63
Oliver D. Mann, D	5,675	37

June 5, 1933

Craig Van Meter, D	27,517	17
George W. Bristow, R	27,250	17
Casper S. Platt, D	27,073	17
Charles A. Shuey, R	26,845	17
Grendel F. Bennett, D	26,701	17
S. Murray Clark, R	26,217	16

November 3, 1936 - Van Meter Vacancy

Grendel F. Bennett, D	50,215	54
V. W. McIntire, R	42,026	46

June 5, 1939

Casper S. Platt, D	27,995	17
George W. Bristow, R	27,778	17
Ben F. Anderson, R	26,852	17
Grendel F. Bennett, D	26,534	16
Howard A. Swallow, R	26,526	16
Wilton A. Carr, D	25,798	16

June 4, 1945

Ben F. Anderson, R	1,844	37
George W. Bristow, R	1,791	35
Casper S. Platt, D	1,416	28

June 4, 1951

Ben F. Anderson, R	17,990	29
Robert F. Cotton, R	17,327	27
John F. Spivey, R	17,278	27
Henry S. Wise, D	10,517	17

June 3, 1957

Harry I. Hannah, R	2,123	33
John F. Spivey, R	2,114	33
Robert F. Cotton, R	2,103	33

November 5, 1974 - Spivey Vacancy

Frank J. Meyer, R	34,839	100

November 5, 1974 - Cotton Vacancy

Ralph S. Pearman, R	33,971	100

<u>November 5, 1974 - Hannah Vacancy</u>

Thomas M. Burke, R	28,378	50
William N. Paris, D	28,196	50

<u>November 4, 1980 - Meyer Vacancy</u>

John P. Meyer, R	44,233	54
Paul T. Manion, D	37,415	46

<u>November 4, 1980 - Burke Vacancy</u>

Paul C. Komada, R	44,864	56
William N. Paris, D	35,613	44

<u>November 4, 1986 - Meyer Vacancy</u>

Rita B. Garman, R	32,985	55
Paul T. Manion, D	27,264	45

<u>November 5, 1996</u>

Dale A. Cini, R	35,831	53
Daniel D. Brown, D	32,177	47

<u>November 3, 1998 - Garman Vacancy</u>

Claudia S. Anderson, R	31,528	60
David J. Ryan, D	21,301	40

<u>November 3, 1998 - Pearman Vacancy</u>

James R. Glenn, R	28,919	52
Daniel D. Brown, D	26,241	48

<u>November 5, 2002 - Komada Vacancy</u>

Mitchell K. Shick, R	29,762	54
C. Steve Ferguson, D	25,399	46

<u>November 2, 2010 - Cini Vacancy</u>

Matthew L. Sullivan, R	45,668	100

D - Democrat
R - Republican

CONTESTED PRIMARY ELECTIONS
(Since 1964)

<u>March 18, 1986 - Democratic</u>

Paul T. Manion	6,833	54
John P. O'Rourke	5,852	46

<u>March 19, 1996 - Democratic</u>

Daniel D. Brown	4,119	56
Michael M. McFatridge	3,257	44

<u>March 19, 1996 - Republican</u>

Dale A. Cini	7,233	51
Claudia S. Anderson	7,050	49

<u>March 17, 1998 - Republican</u>

James R. Glenn	3,766	24
Thomas J. Mellen	3,664	23
Fred Kreckman	3,362	21
Daniel S. Arbogast	2,966	19
Marsha L. Combs	2,144	13

<u>March 19, 2002 - Democratic</u>

C. Steve Ferguson	6,065	61
Stephen R. Ryan	3,923	39

<u>February 2, 2010 - Republican</u>

Matthew L. Sullivan	6,291	39
Frank R. Young	5,079	31
Brian L. Bower	4,436	27
Eric J. Neumann	502	3

SOURCES

Abstract of Election Returns 1818-1850, 582, 583; *Abstract of Election Returns 1850-1862*, 125, 126, 320, 324; *Abstract of Election Returns 1862-1873*, 166, 170; *Abstract of Election Returns 1873-1882*, 7, 8, 164, 165, 249, 250; *Abstract of Election Returns 1882-1912*, 76, 77, 78, 79, 118, 208, 209, 210, 211, 410, 411; State *of Illinois Official Vote Cast at the General Election 1898*, 51; *1910*, 54; *1916*, 53; *1934*, 41; *1936*, 52; *1940*, 54; *1946*, 34; *1952*, 58; *1958*, 53; *1974*, 56; *1980*, 61; *1986*, 111; *1996*, 122; *1998*, 126, 127; *2002*, 145; *Blue Book of the State of Illinois, 1921-1922*, 832; *1929-1930*, 902, 905; *State of Illinois Official Vote Cast at the General Primary Election 1986*, 109; *1996*, 197; *1998*, 149; *2002*, 158; www.elections.state.il.us, 2/2/10, 11/2/10.

CLARK COUNTY
COUNTY JUDGE

<u>November 6, 1849</u>

Stephen Archer	1,177	100

<u>December 9, 1853</u>

John Bartlett	947	57
Sebastian C. Fox	711	43

November 3, 1857
William C. Whitlock   1,483   100

November 5, 1861
William C. Whitlock   1,414   71
William Ramsey   577   29

November 7, 1865
William C. Whitlock   970   51
Burns Archer   928   49

November 2, 1869
William R. Griffith   1,192   69
Burns Archer   525   31

November 4, 1873
Justin Harlan   1,680   51
William R. Griffith   1,600   49

November 6, 1877
William R. Griffith   1,735   49
Justin Harlan   1,556   44
Joseph L. Allison   277   8

November 7, 1882
Ethan A. Sutton   2,178   50
Benson Martin   1,918   44
Joseph A. Hearse   231   5
Levi Watson   69   2

November 2, 1886
Henry Gasaway   2,260   49
Walter Bartlett   2,240   49
T. C. Martin   66   1

November 4, 1890
Henry Gasaway   1,968   41
H. M. Andrews   1,408   29
J. F. Hudson   1,462   30

November 6, 1894
William T. Hollenbeck   2,526   49
Harry M. Janney   2,066   40
S. S. Dixon   432   8
James A. Kelly   115   2

November 8, 1898
J. C. Perdue   2,872   52
U. R. Gard   2,486   45
Thomas M. Cooper   174   3

November 4, 1902
Everett Connelly   2,823   52
J. Q. Snedeker   2,463   46
L. C. Snavely   97   2

November 6, 1906
Hershel R. Snavely   2,525   51
Harry J. Buxbaum   2,333   47
W. C. Grover   93   2

November 8, 1910
Hershel R. Snavely   2,595   53
Edwin D. Jones   2,331   47

November 3, 1914
A. L. Ruffner   2,495   50
Harry M. Janney   2,318   47
John J. Arney   165   3

November 5, 1918
Edward Pearce   2,437   52
Charles A. Purdunn   2,258   48

November 7, 1922
Harry M. Janney, D   4,091   51
Edward Pearce, R   3,957   49

November 2, 1926
Jed Gard, D   4,011   54
John J. Arney, R   3,463   46

November 4, 1930
Jed Gard, D   4,603   55
Claude W. McDaniel, R   3,838   45

November 6, 1934
C. A. Williams, D   4,974   52
Theodore Thompson, R   4,564   48

November 8, 1938
Theodore Thompson, R   4,848   51
C. A. Williams, D   4,722   49

November 3, 1942			November 2, 1880		
Theodore Thompson, R	4,630	58	Thomas L. Orndorff	2,304	50
Fred Gard, D	3,321	42	Henry C. Bell	2,282	50

November 5, 1946			November 4, 1884		
John M. Hollenbeck, R	4,297	55	Newton Tibbs	2,578	54
Caslon K. Bennett, D	3,483	45	Edmund D. Jones	2,205	46

November 7, 1950			November 6, 1888		
John M. Hollenbeck, R	4,835	60	Thomas L. Orndorff	2,700	53
Charles E. McMorris, D	3,272	40	J. C. Pendier	2,365	46
			J. F. Puckner	70	1

November 2, 1954			November 8, 1892		
John M. Hollenbeck, R	4,174	53	Thomas L. Orndorff	2,400	52
Caslon K. Bennett, D	3,773	47	Leander B. Mitchell	2,247	48

November 4, 1958			November 3, 1896		
Zollie O. Arbogast, R	4,258	54	Samuel M. Scholfield	3,047	51
Frederick Kannmacher, D	3,579	46	Fred J. Bartlett	2,912	49

November 6, 1962			November 6, 1900		
Zollie O. Arbogast, R	4,843	100	M. B. Davison	3,064	51
			Thomas L. Orndorff	2,945	49

ASSOCIATE JUDGE

November 5, 1968			November 8, 1904		
Caslon K. Bennett, D	3,776	100	Arthur Poorman	2,860	53
			Edmund D. Jones	2,357	43
			C. F. Tobey	219	4

CIRCUIT JUDGE

November 8, 1988 - Bennett Vacancy

			November 3, 1908		
Zollie O. Arbogast, R	4,783	61	Everett Connelly	3,281	54
Joseph R. Schroeder, D	3,043	39	Miles A. Tipsword	2,756	46

November 6, 1990 - Arbogast Vacancy

			November 5, 1912		
Tracy W. Resch, D	3,510	50	Edmund D. Jones	2,609	50
Dennis E. Simonton, R	3,459	50	Arthur Poorman	2,555	49
			Red Blackwell	91	2

STATE'S ATTORNEY

November 5, 1872			November 7, 1916		
John L. Ryan	1,941	56	Olen R. Clements	3,056	53
Hark D. Hare	1,514	44	Arthur Poorman	2,752	47

November 7, 1876			November 2, 1920		
Thomas L. Orndorff	1,971	48	Everett Connelly, R	5,333	56
John L. Ryan	1,490	36	Olen R. Clements, D	4,173	44
William H. Buckner	654	16			

November 4, 1924
Everett Connelly, R   4,704   52
Harry J. Buxbaum, D   4,424   48

November 6, 1928
Victor C. Miller, R   4,828   53
Grendel F. Bennett, D   4,288   47

November 8, 1932
Carson M. Purdunn, D   5,536   58
Victor C. Miller, R   3,936   42

November 3, 1936
John M. Hollenbeck, R   5,626   51
Carson M. Purdunn, D   5,467   49

November 5, 1940
Claude W. McDaniel, R   5,813   55
Caslon K. Bennett, D   4,711   45

November 7, 1944
Claude W. McDaniel, R   5,501   62
Harry J. Buxbaum, D   3,335   38

November 2, 1948
Claude W. McDaniel, R   4,616   58
Harry J. Buxbaum, D   3,356   42

November 4, 1952
William H. Downey, D   4,778   52
Claude W. McDaniel, R   4,426   48

November 6, 1956
Omer T. Shawler, R   5,386   100

November 8, 1960
Omer T. Shawler, R   5,036   100

November 3, 1964
Omer T. Shawler, R   4,957   100

November 5, 1968
Omer T. Shawler, R   5,059   100

November 7, 1972
Omer T. Shawler, R   5,380   100

November 2, 1976
Tracy W. Resch, D   4,856   58
Randolph M. Rich, R   3,517   42

November 4, 1980
Tracy W. Resch, D   5,421   100

November 2, 1982
David W. Lewis, R   5,044   100

November 6, 1984
David W. Lewis, R   4,659   56
Paul E. Wieck, D   3,604   44

November 8, 1988
David W. Lewis, R   5,448   100

November 3, 1992
David W. Lewis, R   5,570   100

November 5, 1996
David W. Lewis, R   4,866   100

November 7, 2000
David W. Lewis, R   5,531   100

November 5, 2002
Dennis E. Simonton, R   5,089   100

November 2, 2004
Dennis E. Simonton, R   6,126   100

November 4, 2008
Dennis E. Simonton, R   6,913   100

D - Democrat
R – Republican

CONTESTED PRIMARY ELECTIONS
(Since 1930)
COUNTY JUDGE
April 8, 1930 - Republican
Claude W. McDaniel   1,869   68
Edward Pearce   872   32

April 10, 1934 - Democratic
C. A. Williams   2,465   63
Fred Gard   1,424   37

James R. Glenn

April 10, 1934 - Republican

Theodore Thompson	1,472	57
Lawrence Hollenbeck	673	26
John D. Reece	437	17

April 14, 1942 - Democratic

Fred Gard	987	62
Charles E. McMorris	614	38

April 9, 1946 - Republican

John M. Hollenbeck	1,200	53
Theodore Thompson	1,051	47

April 11, 1950 - Republican

John M. Hollenbeck	1,207	56
Theodore Thompson	941	44

April 13, 1954 - Republican

John M. Hollenbeck	1,983	76
Walter E. Cork	628	24

April 8, 1958 - Republican

Zollie O. Arbogast	1,371	58
John M. Hollenbeck	988	42

CIRCUIT JUDGE

March 20, 1990 - Democratic

Tracy W. Resch	937	58
Joseph R. Schroeder	681	42

March 20, 1990 - Republican

Dennis E. Simonton	1,220	50
David W. Lewis	1,209	50

STATE'S ATTORNEY

April 12, 1932 - Democratic

Carson M. Purdunn	1,823	55
Grendel F. Bennett	1,512	45

April 9, 1940 - Democratic

Caslon K. Bennett	804	77
Jerry Middleton	245	23

April 13, 1948 - Republican

Claude W. McDaniel	1,234	55
Charles F. McNary	1,021	45

April 8, 1952 - Republican

Claude W. McDaniel	1,584	54
Henri I. Ripstra	1,329	46

March 19, 1996 - Republican

David W. Lewis	1,117	60
Perry D. Baird	741	40

SOURCES

Abstract of Election Returns 1818-1850, 592; *Abstract of Election Returns 1850-1862*, 187, 296; *Abstract of Election Returns 1862-1873*, 107, 251, 425; *Abstract of Election Returns 1873-1882*, 20, 140, 175, 309; *Abstract of Election Returns 1882-1912*, 7, 59, 105, 165, 223, 267, 316, 367, 410, 459, 502, 552, 5, 30, 50, 72, 92, 120, 143, 163, 182, 205, 225, 245, 264, 287, 304, 324, 341; *Abstract of Votes for County Officers Cast in the County of Clark and State of Illinois, at the Election Held in said County, on 12/9/1853, 4/12/1932, 4/10/1934, 4/9/1940, 11/5/1940, 11/3/1942, 11/7/1944, 11/5/1946, 11/2/1948, 11/7/1950, 11/4/1952, 11/2/1954, 11/6/1956, 11/4/1958, 11/8/1960, 11/6/1962, 11/3/1964, 11/5/1968, 11/7/1972, 11/2/1976, 11/4/1980*; *State of Illinois Official Vote Cast at the General Election 1968*, 72; *1988*, 115-116; *1990*, 118-119; *Clark County Democrat 4/16/30*, 4, *4/22/36*, 6, *4/22/42*, 4, *4/17/46*, 4, *4/21/48*, 9, *4/19/50*, 1, *4/10/52*, 1, *4/15/54*, 1, *11/15/56*, 2, *4/17/58*, 1; *Marshall Independent 11/4/82*, 1, *11/8/84*, 6, *11/10/88*, 1, *11/7/02*, 12: *State of Illinois Official Vote Cast at the General Primary Election 1990*, 145; Records of Clark County Clerk, Bill Downey and staff (2010).

COLES COUNTY
COUNTY JUDGE

November 6, 1849

William W. Bishop	619	58
Thomas A. Marshall	445	42

November 8, 1853

William W. Bishop		(No Record)

November 3, 1857
Gideon Edwards	736	41
G. C. Harding	626	35
William W. Bishop	420	24

November 5, 1861
Gideon Edwards	1,464	56
John A. Boyd	1,149	44

May 17, 1864
Joshua P. Cooper	665	57
William Ricketts	507	43

November 7, 1865
McHenry Brooks	1,525	58
Joseph Edmon	960	37
Joshua P. Cooper	127	5

November 2, 1869
Abner M. Peterson	1,700	61
W. C. Cunningham	1,066	39

November 4, 1873
William E. Adams	1,982	58
Joseph Edmon	1,324	39
Francis A. Allison	127	4

November 6, 1877
James R. Cunningham	2,402	49
William E. Adams	2,277	46
Adam Whitmer	220	4

November 7, 1882
Charles Bennett	2,907	49
James R. Cunningham	2,901	49
Samuel A. Reed	68	1

November 2, 1886
Lapsley C. Henley	3,150	50
Adolf Sumerlin	3,030	48
J. R. Hobart	86	1

November 4, 1890
Lapsley C. Henley	3,505	49
John F. Scott	3,481	49
Jackson A. Colby	135	2

November 6, 1894
Sumner S. Anderson	3,829	53
A. J. Fryer	2,909	40
John M. Hayes	387	5
James Cowton	136	2

November 8, 1898
John P. Harrah	3,716	50
John F. Scott	3,667	49
Charles Bishop	82	1
Adam Whitmer	40	1

November 4, 1902
T. N. Cofer	4,078	55
William H. Crum	3,185	43
J. R. Hobart	110	1

November 6, 1906
T. N. Cofer	3,894	53
John P. Harrah	3,404	47

November 8, 1910
John P. Harrah	3,356	51
Charles Wallace	3,188	49

November 3, 1914
John P. Harrah	3,503	51
Charles Wallace	3,358	49

November 5, 1918
John P. Harrah	3,612	56
H. P. Cofer	2,895	44

November 7, 1922
J. B. Lane, R	6,847	52
J. F. Willingham, D	6,229	48

November 2, 1926
J. B. Lane, R	5,593	50
Charles Wallace, D	5,539	50

November 4, 1930
John T. Kincaid, R	6,285	51
Charles Wallace, D	6,135	49

November 6, 1934
John T. Kincaid, R	8,617	53
Miles A. Tipsword, D	7,637	47

November 8, 1938
John T. Kincaid, R	8,779	54
Carus S. Icenogle, D	7,564	46

November 3, 1942
John T. Kincaid, R	7,919	55
Kenneth Moss, D	6,537	45

November 5, 1946
John T. Kincaid, R	7,421	52
Jack Austin, D	6,735	48

November 7, 1950
William J. Sunderman, R	9,344	57
Ralph E. Suddes, D	7,072	43

November 2, 1954
William J. Sunderman, R	8,564	60
Kenneth A. Green, D	5,709	40

November 4, 1958
William J. Sunderman, R	7,902	52
William K. Kidwell, D	7,153	48

November 6, 1962
William J. Sunderman, R	11,178	100

CITY JUDGE - MATTOON

January 25, 1898
James F. Hughes	1,007	54
Adolf Sumerlin	874	46

January 14, 1902
Lapsley C. Henley	933	51
James L. Scott	881	49

January 9, 1906
Horace S. Clark	936	79
Duncan T. McIntyre	249	21

January 11, 1910
John C. McNutt	789	42
George D. Wilson	599	32
James L. Scott	455	24
J. J. Ashworth	43	2

January 13, 1914
John C. McNutt	892	64
Adolf Sumerlin	506	36

January 8, 1918
John C. McNutt	754	55
Isaac B. Craig	619	45

January 10, 1922
Isaac B. Craig, D	1,706	54
John C. McNutt, R	1,430	46

January 12, 1926
Clarence H. Douglas, R	198	100

January 21, 1930
Clarence H. Douglas, R	1,324	53
James Vause, D	1,193	47

January 21, 1936
Jacob Berkowitz, D	2,293	57
Charles H. Fletcher, R	1,748	43

January 20, 1942
Jacob Berkowitz	2,074	72
Charles H. Fletcher	823	28

January 20, 1948
Jacob Berkowitz	249	100

January 19, 1954
Jacob Berkowitz	232	100

January 19, 1960
Jacob Berkowitz	234	100

CITY JUDGE - CHARLESTON

September 6, 1910
Charles A. Shuey	571	49
T. N. Cofer	499	42
A. J. Fryer	107	9

September 1, 1914
Charles A. Quackenbush	727	61
Miles A. Tipsword	468	39

September 3, 1918
John T. Kincaid 453 59
Miles A. Tipsword 321 41

September 5, 1922
Ben F. Anderson, R 1,104 59
T. N. Cofer, D 776 41

September 7, 1926
Ben F. Anderson, R 1,225 52
Robert G. Hammond, D 1,143 48

September 2, 1930
Herbert S. Anderson, R 1,418 52
T. N. Cofer, D 1,296 48

September 1, 1936
C. Wade Barrick, R 1,839 61
Alton B. Cofer, D 1,184 39

September 1, 1942
C. Wade Barrick, R 1,318 67
Alton B. Cofer, D 647 33

September 7, 1948
C. Wade Barrick 1,176 71
Alton B. Cofer 483 29

September 7, 1954
C. Wade Barrick 749 72
Thomas M. Burke 297 28

September 6, 1960
Jack H. Anderson 1,041 52
Jack Austin 948 48

CIRCUIT JUDGE
November 7, 1978 - Berkowitz Vacancy
Joseph R. Spitz, R 9,558 100

November 6, 1990 - Sunderman Vacancy
Ashton C. Waller, R 12,626 100

November 3, 1992 - Spitz Vacancy
Gary W. Jacobs, R 17,393 100

November 2, 2004 - Waller Vacancy
Teresa K. Righter, R 14,069 65
William R. Tapella, D 7,455 35

STATE'S ATTORNEY
November 5, 1872
James W. Craig 2,680 50
Alexander P. Dunbar 2,649 50

November 7, 1876
Robert M. Gray 3,006 51
Isaac B. Craig 2,852 49

November 2, 1880
Samuel M. Leitch 3,024 50
James K. Rardin 2,965 50

November 4, 1884
Samuel M. Leitch 3,404 52
George C. Mathes 3,086 48

November 6, 1888
John H. Marshall 3,465 51
James R. Cunningham 3,257 48
John C. Brooks 125 2

November 8, 1892 *
John S. Hall 3,652 48
John H. Marshall 3,648 48
Jackson A. Colby 269 4

November 3, 1896
Emery Andrews 4,380 51
Charles C. Lee 4,098 48
Thomas D. Davis 50 1

November 6, 1900
John F. Voigt 4,780 56
E. D. Elder 3,827 44

November 8, 1904
John C. McNutt 4,606 52
Anderson Stewart 3,801 43
Jacob J. Hudson 243 3
John Cauthon 133 2

<table>
<tr><td colspan="3"><u>November 3, 1908</u></td><td colspan="3"><u>November 6, 1956</u></td></tr>
<tr><td>Robert G. Hammond</td><td>4,273</td><td>51</td><td>Thomas M. Burke, R</td><td>10,175</td><td>53</td></tr>
<tr><td>John C. McNutt</td><td>4,158</td><td>49</td><td>Hugh Harwood, D</td><td>9,199</td><td>47</td></tr>
<tr><td colspan="3"><u>November 5, 1912</u></td><td colspan="3"><u>November 8, 1960</u></td></tr>
<tr><td>Robert G. Hammond</td><td>4,028</td><td>56</td><td>Ralph D. Glenn, R</td><td>10,638</td><td>52</td></tr>
<tr><td>Sumner S. Anderson</td><td>3,118</td><td>44</td><td>William K. Kidwell, D</td><td>9,822</td><td>48</td></tr>
<tr><td colspan="3"><u>November 7, 1916</u></td><td colspan="3"><u>November 3, 1964</u></td></tr>
<tr><td>Emery Andrews</td><td>4,522</td><td>50</td><td>Ralph D. Glenn, R</td><td>11,343</td><td>100</td></tr>
<tr><td>Ira Powell</td><td>4,494</td><td>50</td><td></td><td></td><td></td></tr>
<tr><td></td><td></td><td></td><td colspan="3"><u>November 5, 1968</u></td></tr>
<tr><td colspan="3"><u>November 2, 1920</u></td><td>L. Stanton Dotson, R</td><td>11,151</td><td>59</td></tr>
<tr><td>Charles H. Fletcher, R</td><td>8,887</td><td>62</td><td>John J. McCarthy, D</td><td>7,828</td><td>41</td></tr>
<tr><td>Ira Powell, D</td><td>5,534</td><td>38</td><td></td><td></td><td></td></tr>
<tr><td></td><td></td><td></td><td colspan="3"><u>November 7, 1972</u></td></tr>
<tr><td colspan="3"><u>November 4, 1924</u></td><td>John J. McCarthy, D</td><td>10,977</td><td>52</td></tr>
<tr><td>Charles H. Fletcher, R</td><td>7,987</td><td>53</td><td>L. Stanton Dotson, R</td><td>10,311</td><td>48</td></tr>
<tr><td>Carl D. Kiger, D</td><td>7,081</td><td>47</td><td></td><td></td><td></td></tr>
<tr><td></td><td></td><td></td><td colspan="3"><u>November 5, 1974</u></td></tr>
<tr><td colspan="3"><u>November 6, 1928</u></td><td>Paul C. Komada, R</td><td>6,734</td><td>52</td></tr>
<tr><td>C. M. Heinlein, R</td><td>10,650</td><td>68</td><td>Bobby F. Sanders, D</td><td>6,183</td><td>48</td></tr>
<tr><td>Miles A. Tipsword, D</td><td>5,053</td><td>32</td><td></td><td></td><td></td></tr>
<tr><td></td><td></td><td></td><td colspan="3"><u>November 2, 1976</u></td></tr>
<tr><td colspan="3"><u>November 8, 1932</u></td><td>Paul C. Komada, R</td><td>10,850</td><td>58</td></tr>
<tr><td>Jewell I. Dilsaver, D</td><td>10,323</td><td>58</td><td>David R. Moreland, D</td><td>7,711</td><td>42</td></tr>
<tr><td>C. M. Heinlein, R</td><td>7,459</td><td>42</td><td></td><td></td><td></td></tr>
<tr><td></td><td></td><td></td><td colspan="3"><u>November 4, 1980</u></td></tr>
<tr><td colspan="3"><u>November 3, 1936</u></td><td>Nancy W. Owen, R</td><td>12,166</td><td>61</td></tr>
<tr><td>Jewell I. Dilsaver, D</td><td>11,782</td><td>58</td><td>Lonnie L. Lutz, D</td><td>7,875</td><td>39</td></tr>
<tr><td>C. M. Heinlein, R</td><td>8,507</td><td>42</td><td></td><td></td><td></td></tr>
<tr><td></td><td></td><td></td><td colspan="3"><u>November 6, 1984</u></td></tr>
<tr><td colspan="3"><u>November 5, 1940</u></td><td>Nancy W. Owen, R</td><td>11,903</td><td>57</td></tr>
<tr><td>William K. Kidwell, D</td><td>11,596</td><td>55</td><td>James B. Zimarowski, D</td><td>9,102</td><td>43</td></tr>
<tr><td>Charles H. Fletcher, R</td><td>9,599</td><td>45</td><td></td><td></td><td></td></tr>
<tr><td></td><td></td><td></td><td colspan="3"><u>November 8, 1988</u></td></tr>
<tr><td colspan="3"><u>November 7, 1944</u></td><td>Nancy W. Owen, R</td><td>14,166</td><td>100</td></tr>
<tr><td>William K. Kidwell, D</td><td>9,033</td><td>51</td><td></td><td></td><td></td></tr>
<tr><td>William J. Sunderman, R</td><td>8,768</td><td>49</td><td colspan="3"><u>November 3, 1992</u></td></tr>
<tr><td></td><td></td><td></td><td>C. Steve Ferguson, D</td><td>11,762</td><td>54</td></tr>
<tr><td colspan="3"><u>November 2, 1948</u></td><td>Mark Novak, R</td><td>9,862</td><td>46</td></tr>
<tr><td>Hugh Harwood, D</td><td>9,112</td><td>55</td><td></td><td></td><td></td></tr>
<tr><td>Orville F. Schoch, R</td><td>7,445</td><td>45</td><td colspan="3"><u>November 5, 1996</u></td></tr>
<tr><td></td><td></td><td></td><td>C. Steve Ferguson, D</td><td>11,458</td><td>62</td></tr>
<tr><td colspan="3"><u>November 4, 1952</u></td><td>David S. Stewart, R</td><td>7,077</td><td>38</td></tr>
<tr><td>Hugh Harwood, D</td><td>10,980</td><td>55</td><td></td><td></td><td></td></tr>
<tr><td>H. J. Hasch, R</td><td>8,945</td><td>45</td><td></td><td></td><td></td></tr>
</table>

November 7, 2000

| C. Steve Ferguson, D | 10,553 | 55 |
| Preston Owen, R | 8,803 | 45 |

November 2, 2004

C. Steve Ferguson, D	9,083	42
Rob Miller, R	8,527	39
Todd M. Reardon, I	4,105	19

November 4, 2008

C. Steve Ferguson, D	9,403	42
Paul C. Komada, R	7,531	34
Todd M. Reardon, G	5,365	24

* Result changed by election contest
D - Democrat   I - Independent
R - Republican   G - Green

CONTESTED PRIMARY ELECTIONS
(Since 1930)
COUNTY JUDGE

April 8, 1930 - Democratic

| Charles Wallace | 1,568 | 66 |
| Adolf Sumerlin | 820 | 34 |

April 8, 1930 - Republican

| John T. Kincaid | 3,578 | 54 |
| F. N. Henley | 3,107 | 46 |

April 10, 1934 - Democratic

| Miles A. Tipsword | 2,673 | 53 |
| Jacob Berkowitz | 2,382 | 47 |

April 10, 1934 - Republican

| John T. Kincaid | 3,142 | 53 |
| C. Wade Barrick | 2,776 | 47 |

April 14, 1942 - Democratic

Kenneth Moss	147	55
R. T. Hammond	90	34
Alton B. Cofer	29	11

April 11, 1950 - Republican

| William J. Sunderman | 3,209 | 60 |
| John J. Yelvington | 2,174 | 40 |

CIRCUIT JUDGE

March 20, 1990 - Republican

| Ashton C. Waller | 3,987 | 68 |
| Nancy W. Owen | 1,883 | 32 |

March 17, 1992 - Republican

| Gary W. Jacobs | 4,405 | 79 |
| Priscilla Ebdon | 1,161 | 21 |

STATE'S ATTORNEY

April 12, 1932 - Republican

| C. M. Heinlein | 3,974 | 58 |
| C. Wade Barrick | 2,833 | 42 |

April 13, 1948 - Republican

| Orville F. Schoch | 1,984 | 60 |
| H. J. Hasch | 1,323 | 40 |

April 10, 1956 - Republican

Thomas M. Burke	2,059	44
Orville F. Schoch	1,626	35
H. J. Hasch	1,015	22

April 12, 1960 - Republican

| Ralph D. Glenn | 4,719 | 73 |
| Mervin L. Beil | 1,733 | 27 |

March 18, 1980 - Democratic

| Lonnie L. Lutz | 1,521 | 52 |
| John E. Elder | 1,406 | 48 |

March 18, 1980 - Republican

Nancy W. Owen	3,185	55
James C. Dedman	1,652	28
Rick L. Hobler	972	17

March 17, 1992 - Democratic

| C. Steve Ferguson | 2,940 | 64 |
| Marsha L. Combs | 1,637 | 36 |

February 5, 2008 - Republican

| Paul C. Komada | 2,265 | 50 |
| Duane Deters | 2,249 | 50 |

SOURCES

Abstract of Election Returns 1818-1850, 592; *Abstract of Election Returns 1850-1862*, 188, 296; *Abstract of Election Returns 1862-1873*, 50, 107, 252, 426; *Abstract of Election Returns 1873-1882*, 21, 141, 176, 310; *Abstract of Election Returns 1882-1912*, 8, 60, 106, 166, 224, 268, 318, 368, 411, 460, 503, 553, 5, 31, 50, 73, 93, 121, 144, 163, 184, 205, 226, 246, 265, 287, 304, 324, 342; *Abstract of Votes for County Officers Cast in the County of Coles and State of Illinois, at the Election Held in said County, on 4/8/1930*; *Canvass by Voting Precincts of the Votes Cast at the General Election Held in the County of Coles and State of Illinois on Tuesday*, 11/5/40, 11/3/42, 11/7/44, 11/5/46, 11/2/48, 11/7/50, 11/4/52, 11/2/54, 11/6/56, 11/4/58, 11/8/60, 11/6/62, 11/3/64, 11/5/68, 11/7/72, 11/5/74, 11/2/76; *State of Illinois Official Vote Cast at the General Election 1978*, 83; *1990*, 118-119; *1992*, 149; *2004*, 114; *Mattoon Daily Journal, Gazette, or Journal-Gazette* 1/26/1898, 4, 1/15/02, 1, 1/10/06, 1, 1/12/10, 1, 1/14/14, 1, 1/9/18, 1, 1/11/22, 1, 1/13/26, 5, 1/22/30, 1, 4/13/32, 1, 1/22/36, 1, 1/21/42, 1, 1/21/48, 1, 1/20/54, 12, 1/20/60, 1; *Charleston Daily Courier, Daily News, or Courier-News* 9/7/10, 1, 9/2/14, 1, 9/4/18, 1, 9/6/22, 1, 9/8/26, 1, 9/3/30, 1, 9/2/36, 1, 9/2/42, 1, 9/8/48, 1, 9/8/54, 1, 9/7/60, 1; *Canvass by Voting Precincts of the Votes Cast at the Primary Election Held in the County of Coles and State of Illinois on Tuesday*, 4/10/34, 4/14/42, 4/13/48, 4/11/50, 4/10/56, 4/12/60, 3/18/80, 3/17/92, 2/5/08; *State of Illinois Official Vote Cast at the General Primary Election 1990*, 145; *1992*, 221; Records of Coles County Clerk, Sue Rennels and staff (2010).

CUMBERLAND COUNTY
COUNTY JUDGE

November 6, 1849

James M. Ward	331	66
James Gill	97	19
William M. P. Quinn	73	15

November 8, 1853

William E. Smith	(No Record)

November 3, 1857

William E. Smith	521	51
James M. Ward	502	49

November 5, 1861

Hiram B. Decius	643	57
William E. Smith	481	43

November 8, 1864

Reuben Bloomfield	1,117	65
Michael Ruffner	598	35

November 7, 1865

Reuben Bloomfield	778	69
Meredith B. Ross	343	31

November 2, 1869

Wiley Ross	791	53
A. Kelley	700	47

November 4, 1873

John W. Miller	1,067	56
John Prather	844	44

November 6, 1877

John W. Miller	1,019	53
Norman L. Scranton	894	47

November 7, 1882

Leonidas L. Logan	1,380	54
Thomas Brewer	1,005	39
R. C. Carpenter	160	6

November 2, 1886

Phillip Welshimer	1,790	57
Leonidas L. Logan	1,348	43

November 4, 1890

Leonidas L. Logan	1,713	55
D. S. Hutchison	1,404	45

November 6, 1894

Gershom Monohon	1,746	50
Levi B. Ross	1,663	47
John W. Nudham	116	3

November 8, 1898

Elias M. McPherson	1,891	52
Frank D. Voris	1,729	48

November 4, 1902

Stephen B. Rariden	1,762	51
Gershom Monohon	1,645	47
E. S. Logan	68	2

November 6, 1906

A. L. Ruffner	1,600	49
Stephen B. Rariden	1,590	49
Jacob V. Runkel	84	3

November 8, 1910

Stephen B. Rariden	1,645	53
Irving J. Brown	1,435	47

November 3, 1914

Stephen B. Rariden	1,481	49
Charles M. Connor	1,440	48
J. C. Waldrip	106	4

November 5, 1918

Albert F. Bussard	1,548	54
Levi B. Ross	1,333	46

November 7, 1922

Albert F. Bussard, R	2,810	56
Nelson Tharp, D	2,214	44

November 2, 1926

Albert F. Bussard, R	2,342	51
Wilton A. Carr, D	2,226	49

November 4, 1930

Charles M. Connor, R	2,340	52
Walter C. Greathouse, D	2,198	48

November 6, 1934

Charles M. Connor, R	2,852	51
John M. Connor, D	2,756	49

November 8, 1938

Charles M. Connor, R	2,915	52
Glen D. Neal, D	2,694	48

November 3, 1942

Millard C. Everhart, R	2,634	54
Glen D. Neal, D	2,227	46

November 5, 1946

Millard C. Everhart, R	2,780	60
James Moore, D	1,826	40

November 7, 1950

Millard C. Everhart, R	2,813	58
H. P. Shields, D	2,019	42

November 2, 1954

William J. Hill, D	2,569	51
Millard C. Everhart, R	2,431	49

November 4, 1958

William J. Hill, D	2,843	56
Herman O. Ewart, R	2,263	44

November 6, 1962

William J. Hill, D	2,951	61
H. J. Hasch, R	1,925	39

ASSOCIATE JUDGE

November 8, 1966

James R. Watson, R	2,520	52
Wilton A. Carr, D	2,324	48

CIRCUIT JUDGE

November 6, 1990 - Watson Vacancy

Robert B. Cochonour, R	3,629	100

November 2, 2004 - Cochonour Vacancy

Millard S. Everhart, R	3,005	58
John L. Barger, D	2,191	42

STATE'S ATTORNEY

November 5, 1872

Andrew J. Lee	1,149	50
James Ryan	1,142	50

November 7, 1876

Thomas Warner	1,404	54
Leonidas L. Logan	1,184	46

James R. Glenn

November 2, 1880
William C. Prather   1,476   51
Peter A. Brady   1,401   49

November 4, 1884
Hiram L. Scranton   1,730   54
James B. Atchison   1,491   46

November 6, 1888
William H. McDonald   1,800   55
Andrew J. Lee   1,471   45

November 8, 1892
William H. McDonald   1,822   54
Lyle C. Woods   1,450   44
J. D. Bordon   103   3

November 3, 1896
Smith Misner   2,030   52
Charles M. Connor   1,875   48

November 6, 1900
William H. McDonald   2,040   53
D. B. Green   1,832   47

November 8, 1904
Walter Brewer   1,899   53
Walter C. Greathouse   1,680   47

November 3, 1908
Walter C. Greathouse   1,840   51
Charles M. Connor   1,737   49

November 5, 1912
Walter Brewer   1,612   50
Walter C. Greathouse   1,609   50

November 7, 1916
Glenn Ratcliff   1,914   56
Charles M. Connor   1,518   44

November 2, 1920
Charles C. Eggleston, R   3,080   58
Walter C. Greathouse, D   2,218   42

June 12, 1923
Walter C. Greathouse, D   1,121   53
Charles M. Connor, R   990   47

November 4, 1924
Walter C. Greathouse, D   2,772   52
Charles M. Connor, R   2,590   48

November 6, 1928
Wilton A. Carr, D   2,634   52
Hiram L. Scranton, R   2,470   48

November 8, 1932
Theodore O. Cutright, D   3,007   57
August C. Caylor, R   2,250   43

November 3, 1936
Theodore O. Cutright, D   3,424   55
August C. Caylor, R   2,761   45

November 5, 1940
Walter Brewer, Jr., R   3,583   56
Theodore O. Cutright, D   2,782   44

November 7, 1944
Glen D. Neal, D   2,544   51
J. R. Blomquist, R   2,491   49

November 2, 1948
Glen D. Neal, D   2,589   55
August C. Caylor, R   2,152   45

November 4, 1952
August C. Caylor, R   2,879   53
Glen D. Neal, D   2,594   47

November 6, 1956
Glen D. Neal, D   2,778   52
August C. Caylor, R   2,587   48

November 8, 1960
Glen D. Neal, D   3,102   100

November 3, 1964
Glen D. Neal, D   3,138   60
H. J. Hasch, R   2,082   40

November 5, 1968
Glen D. Neal, D   2,653   100

November 7, 1972

Robert B. Cochonour, R	3,005	56
Theodore O. Cutright, D	2,384	44

November 2, 1976

Robert B. Cochonour, R	2,727	52
Steven P. Seymour, D	2,544	48

November 4, 1980

Daniel S. Arbogast, R	2,834	55
Bobby F. Sanders, D	2,346	45

November 6, 1984

Martin R. Schnorf, R	2,426	53
Richard M. Kash, D	2,177	47

November 8, 1988

Millard S. Everhart, R	3,510	100

November 3, 1992

Millard S. Everhart, R	3,841	100

November 5, 1996

Millard S. Everhart, R	2,606	60
Gregg W. Bonelli, D	1,715	40

November 7, 2000

Millard S. Everhart, R	3,023	63
Gregg W. Bonelli, D	1,785	37

November 2, 2004

Barry E. Schaefer, R	3,016	58
Shon A. Park, D	2,193	42

November 4, 2008

Barry E. Schaefer, R	3,823	75
Mervin Wolfe, D	1,292	25

D - Democrat
R - Republican

CONTESTED PRIMARY ELECTIONS
(Since 1930)
COUNTY JUDGE
April 8, 1930 - Republican

Charles M. Connor	903	59
Hiram L. Scranton	639	41

April 10, 1934 - Democratic

John M. Connor	1,592	72
Charles E. Hicks	607	28

April 10, 1934 - Republican

Charles M. Connor	1,127	60
A. L. Ruffner	736	40

April 12, 1938 - Democratic

Glen D. Neal	305	50
Marion Underwood	280	46
L. W. MacNeil	19	3

April 14, 1942 - Republican

Millard C. Everhart	211	59
Charles M. Connor	120	34
J. C. Lohrman	27	8

April 9, 1946 - Republican

Millard C. Everhart	895	61
Hollis Wright	564	39

April 8, 1958 - Democratic

William J. Hill	1,148	83
Earl Trimble	232	17

CIRCUIT JUDGE
March 20, 1990 - Republican

Robert B. Cochonour	1,178	67
Glenn A. Braden	585	33

March 16, 2004 - Democratic

John L. Barger	546	53
Brian R. Reed	319	31
Kenneth R. Gano	169	16

STATE'S ATTORNEY
April 12, 1932 - Democratic

Theodore O. Cutright	708	35
Wilton A. Carr	669	33
Glen D. Neal	631	31

April 14, 1936 - Democratic *

Glen D. Neal	1,374	50
Theodore O. Cutright	1,371	50

April 10, 1956 - Democratic

Glen D. Neal	1,074	62
Wilton A. Carr	650	38

April 12, 1960 - Democratic

Glen D. Neal	899	61
Charles W. Grisamore	583	39

March 16, 1976 - Democratic

Steven P. Seymour	816	37
Marilyn Resch	714	32
Bobby F. Sanders	691	31

March 16, 2004 - Republican

Barry E. Schaefer	569	72
Scott S. Matteson	223	28

February 5, 2008 - Republican

Barry E. Schaefer	755	62
John E. Longwell	456	38

* Result changed by election contest

SOURCES

Abstract of Election Returns 1818-1850, 593; *Abstract of Election Returns 1850-1862*, 188, 296; *Abstract of Election Returns 1862-1873*, 90, 108, 253, 427; *Abstract of Election Returns 1873-1882*, 21, 142, 177, 311; *Abstract of Election Returns 1882-1912*, 11, 61, 102, 169, 226, 273, 322, 371, 416, 465, 508, 558, 8, 33, 52, 75, 95, 122, 145, 164, 185, 201, 206, 228, 246, 267, 288, 306, 325, 343; *Abstract of Votes for County Officers Cast in the County of Cumberland and State of Illinois, at the Election Held in said County, on 4/10/1934, 11/5/1940, 11/3/1942, 11/7/1944, 11/5/1946, 11/2/1948, 11/7/1950, 11/4/1952, 11/2/1954, 11/6/1956, 11/4/1958, 11/8/1960, 11/6/1962, 11/3/1964, 11/5/1968, 11/7/1972, 3/16/76, 11/2/1976, 11/4/1980*; State of Illinois Official Vote Cast at the General Election 1966, 61; *1990*, 118-119; *2004*, 114; *Toledo Democrat 4/10/30*, 1, *4/14/32*, 1, *4/16/36*, 5, *4/14/38*, 1, *4/16/42*, 2, *4/11/46*, 1, *4/12/56*, 1, *4/10/58*, 1, *4/14/60*, 1, *11/8/84*, 7, *11/10/88*, 5, *11/19/92*, 5;

State of Illinois Official Vote Cast at the General Primary Election 1990, 145; *2004*, 114; Records of Cumberland County Clerk, Julie Gentry and staff (2010).

EDGAR COUNTY
COUNTY JUDGE

November 6, 1849

Samuel Connelly	676	100

November 8, 1853

James Steele	(No Record)	

November 3, 1857

A. B. Austin	1,722	100

November 5, 1861

George K. Larkin	1,369	51
John J. Fouts	1,333	49

November 7, 1865

Andrew Y. Trogdon	1,689	53
Henry Tanner	1,477	47

November 2, 1869

Robert B. Lamon	2,086	53
J. B. Hannah	1,820	47

November 4, 1873

Robert B. Lamon	2,176	53
Henry Tanner	1,960	47

November 6, 1877

Andrew Y. Trogdon	2,619	51
Robert B. Lamon	2,510	49

November 7, 1882

Andrew Y. Trogdon	3,060	50
Henry Tanner	3,022	50

November 2, 1886

Andrew J. Hunter	3,186	51
James F. Van Vorhees	2,866	46
Moses Marks	155	2

November 4, 1890
Andrew J. Hunter	3,339	51
Andrew Y. Trogdon	3,053	47
George Ringland	120	2

November 6, 1894
Erasmus G. Rose	3,377	49
Stephen I. Headley	3,289	47
Joseph Blackburn	144	2
Allen Sly	129	2

November 8, 1898
Stephen I. Headley	3,540	49
George M. Jeter	3,472	49
Harry C. Clark	94	1
Mac G. Hudson	49	1

November 4, 1902
Walter S. Lamon	3,875	53
Joel W. Nye	3,350	46
Samuel F. Hannold	112	2

November 6, 1906
Walter S. Lamon	3,568	50
Erasmus G. Rose	3,328	47
F. M. Walthall	193	3

November 8, 1910
Daniel V. Dayton	3,479	50
Fred Rhoads	3,248	47
M. I. Delap	119	2
L. F. Kleinfelter	51	1

November 3, 1914
Daniel V. Dayton	3,691	51
Jay Fay Cusick	2,737	38
Carvil H. Laughlin	733	10
L. K. Howerton	65	1

November 5, 1918
Daniel V. Dayton	3,169	55
J. E. Bacon	2,621	45

November 7, 1922
Paul B. Lauher, D	6,462	55
Edward A. Schroeder, R	5,226	45

November 2, 1926
Paul B. Lauher, D	6,230	60
C. Howard Hoult, R	4,178	40

November 4, 1930
Paul B. Lauher, D	6,532	55
Guy Hicks, R	5,394	45

November 6, 1934
Paul B. Lauher, D	7,873	60
Charles F. Tym, R	5,278	40

November 8, 1938
Paul B. Lauher, D	7,378	58
Robert L. Bane, R	5,420	42

November 3, 1942
Paul B. Lauher, D	5,528	53
Frances Alexander, R	4,818	47

November 5, 1946
Howard T. Ruff, R	6,326	61
Roger Fruin, D	4,068	39

November 7, 1950
Howard T. Ruff, R	6,797	61
John R. Moss, D	4,323	39

November 2, 1954
Howard T. Ruff, R	6,987	63
Frank E. Fox, D	4,143	37

November 4, 1958
Howard T. Ruff, R	5,115	52
Paul B. Lauher, D	4,701	48

November 6, 1962
Howard T. Ruff, R	5,693	53
John R. Moss, D	4,981	47

CIRCUIT JUDGE

November 5, 1974 - Ruff Vacancy
Carl A. Lund, R	5,149	100

November 8, 1988 - Lund Vacancy
Richard E. Scott, R	7,028	100

November 7, 2000 - Scott Vacancy
H. Dean Andrews, R   6,745   100

November 4, 2008 - Andrews Vacancy
Steven L. Garst, R   7,189   100

STATE'S ATTORNEY

November 5, 1872
Henry S. Tanner   2,322   51
Andrew Y. Trogdon   2,271   49

November 7, 1876
Henry S. Tanner   3,104   54
John G. Wooley   2,602   46

November 2, 1880
John W. Shepherd   3,048   51
George E. Bacon   2,888   49

November 4, 1884
John W. Shepherd   3,319   54
Jason W. Howell   2,858   46

November 6, 1888
Frank P. Hardy   3,173   49
Joseph E. Dyas   3,104   48
John P. Burchit   148   2

November 8, 1892
Alfred Tanner   3,173   48
Willis H. Clinton   3,173   48
John F. Boyer   180   3
Dillard N. Johnson   150   2

November 3, 1896
Harry H. Van Sellar 3,824   51
Sidney E. Eads   3,691   49
Charles S. Myers   49   1

November 6, 1900
John W. Murphy   3,890   51
John W. Doak   3,652   48
John K. Failing   117   2

November 8, 1904
Walter V. Arbuckle   3,713   50
George A. Van Dyke   3,616   49
J. C. Cox   34   0

November 3, 1908
Richard S. Dyas   3,794   51
Stewart W. Kincaid   3,398   46
Dillard N. Johnson   172   2
W. L. Estes   45   1

November 5, 1912
Wilber H. Hickman   3,526   53
Richard S. Dyas   2,995   45
Carl Buckler   149   2

November 7, 1916
Wilber H. Hickman   3,793   53
Jay Fay Cusick   3,311   47

November 2, 1920
George W. Bristow, R 6,694   54
Paul B. Lauher, D   5,716   46

November 4, 1924
Walter S. Lamon, D   6,575   55
George W. Bristow, R 5,303   45

November 6, 1928
Charles F. Tym, R   6,591   53
Walter S. Lamon, D   5,812   47

November 8, 1932
Walter S. Lamon, D   7,630   57
Grant Johnson, R   5,678   43

November 3, 1936
Ward E. Dillavou, R   7,425   51
Walter S. Lamon, D   7,112   49

November 5, 1940
Ward E. Dillavou, R   7,610   53
William L. Roller, D 6,836   47

<u>November 7, 1944</u>
Ward E. Dillavou, R   6,621   57
Joseph E. Cooper, D   4,955   43

<u>November 2, 1948</u>
Wilson Dwyer, D   6,350   57
Ward E. Dillavou, R   4,887   43

<u>November 4, 1952</u>
Wayne S. Jones, R   8,611   68
Wilson Dwyer, D   4,006   32

<u>November 6, 1956</u>
Wayne S. Jones, R   7,140   59
John R. Moss, D   4,933   41

<u>November 8, 1960</u>
Ralph S. Pearman, R   7,340   100

<u>November 3, 1964</u>
Carl A. Lund, R   6,682   100

<u>November 5, 1968</u>
Charles J. Gramlich, R   6,903   100

<u>November 7, 1972</u>
Arthur A. Jones, R   7,237   100

<u>November 2, 1976</u>
Peter T. Dole, R   6,930   100

<u>November 4, 1980</u>
Michael M. McFatridge, D 5,174   50
Peter T. Dole, R   5,155   50

<u>November 6, 1984</u>
Michael M. McFatridge, D 6,325   100

<u>November 8, 1988</u>
Michael M. McFatridge, D 6,313   100

<u>November 3, 1992</u>
Allan F. Lolie, D   5,687   59
Allen A. Bell, R   3,970   41

<u>November 5, 1996</u>
Matthew L. Sullivan, R   4,147   51
Allan F. Lolie, D   4,052   49

<u>November 7, 2000</u>
Matthew L. Sullivan, R   6,178   100

<u>November 2, 2004</u>
Matthew L. Sullivan, R   6,633   100

<u>November 4, 2008</u>
Matthew L. Sullivan, R   6,695   100

<u>November 2, 2010</u>
Mark R. Isaf, R   5,953   100

D - Democrat
R - Republican

CONTESTED PRIMARY ELECTIONS
(Since 1930)
COUNTY JUDGE
<u>April 10, 1934 - Republican</u>
Charles F. Tym   1,318   63
Frank W. Scanling   768   37

<u>April 12, 1938 - Democratic</u>
Paul B. Lauher   3,938   81
Curtis H. Anderson   900   19

<u>April 9, 1946 - Republican</u>
Howard T. Ruff   2,044   67
Guy Hicks   997   33

<u>April 13, 1954 - Democratic</u>
Frank E. Fox   197   63
John R. Moss   114   37

<u>April 10, 1962 - Republican</u>
Howard T. Ruff   2,308   54
Carl A. Lund   1,931   46

CIRCUIT JUDGE
<u>February 5, 2008 - Republican</u>
Steven L. Garst   2,451   78
Bruce Baber   710   22

James R. Glenn

STATE'S ATTORNEY

April 12, 1932 - Republican

Grant Johnson	2,227	52
Charles F. Tym	2,066	48

April 14, 1936 - Democratic

Walter S. Lamon	3,023	58
Hartman Schwartz	2,189	42

April 9, 1940 - Democratic

William L. Roller	3,618	88
Hartman Schwartz	483	12

April 13, 1948 - Republican

Ward E. Dillavou	1,420	62
Grant Johnson	853	38

April 8, 1952 - Republican

Wayne S. Jones	2,154	51
James C. Stanfield	2,079	49

March 17, 1992 - Republican

Allen A. Bell	1,370	51
Karen L. Burkybile	1,294	49

SOURCES

Abstract of Election Returns 1818-1850, 594; *Abstract of Election Returns 1850-1862*, 188, 298; *Abstract of Election Returns 1862-1873*, 109, 254, 428; *Abstract of Election Returns 1873-1882*, 22, 143, 178, 312; *Abstract of Election Returns 1882-1912*, 13, 63, 110, 171, 228, 275, 324, 372, 418, 466, 511, 559, 9, 33, 53, 75, 96, 122, 146, 165, 186, 207, 228, 247, 268, 288, 307, 325, 344; *Canvass by Voting Precincts of the Votes Cast at the General Election Held in the County of Edgar and State of Illinois on Tuesday, 11/5/40, 11/3/42, 11/7/44, 11/5/46, 11/2/48, 11/7/50, 11/4/52, 11/2/54, 11/6/56, 11/4/58, 11/8/60, 11/6/62, 11/3/64, 11/5/68, 11/7/72, 11/2/76*; *State of Illinois Official Vote Cast at the General Election 1974*, 56; *1988*, 115-116; *2000*, 95-96; www.elections.state. il.us, 2/5/08, 11/4/08; www.libertysystemsllc. com/results/VoteTracker.aspx?county=Edgar; *Paris Daily Beacon-News 4/18/32, 2, 4/13/34, 2, 4/18/36, 2, 4/15/38, 2; Canvass by Voting Precincts of the Votes Cast at the Primary Election Held in the County of Edgar and State of Illinois on Tuesday, 4/9/40, 4/9/46, 4/13/48, 4/8/52, 4/13/54, 4/10/62, 3/17/92*; Records of Edgar County Clerk, Rebecca R. Kraemer and staff (2010).

VERMILION COUNTY
COUNTY JUDGE

November 6, 1849

Guy Merrill	1,075	100

November 8, 1853

Guy Merrill	406	76
Benjamin Stewart	131	24

November 3, 1857

Norman D. Palmer	714	53
Joseph Peters	632	47

November 16, 1858

Joseph Peters	431	64
Hamilton White	245	36

November 5, 1861

Joseph Peters	1,038	38
Daniel Clapp	918	33
John N. Drake	800	29

January 6, 1863

Robert B. Lamon	903	56
M. D. Hawes	709	44

November 7, 1865

Daniel Clapp	1,411	59
Robert B. Lamon	971	41

November 2, 1869

Raymond W. Hanford	1,239	76
A. H. T. Bryant	397	24

November 4, 1873

Raymond W. Hanford	2,014	65
Addison N. Davis	1,065	35

November 6, 1877

Raymond W. Hanford	2,441	61
Elias S. Terry	1,555	39

November 7, 1882
David D. Evans   5,949   100

November 2, 1886
David D. Evans   5,192   59
George W. Salmans   3,668   41

November 4, 1890
John G. Thompson   5,740   53
David D. Evans   4,648   43
Charles V. Guy   351   3

November 6, 1894
John G. Thompson   6,022   65
George W. Salmans   2,839   31
Hiram K. Catlett   413   4

July 27, 1897
Morton W. Thompson   1,340   99
George R. Tilton   16   1

November 8, 1898
Morton W. Thompson   6,040   100

November 4, 1902
S. Murray Clark   6,382   64
William H. Dwyer   2,803   28
George S. Hoff   486   5
William Topham   321   3

November 6, 1906
Isaac A. Love   7,799   71
Jay T. Michaels   2,252   21
Clark J. Phetteplace   876   8

July 7, 1909
Lawrence T. Allen   4,796   100

November 8, 1910
Lawrence T. Allen   8,314   66
C. R. Hill   3,368   27
Lynden F. Lascell   536   4
W. B. Braucher   405   3

November 3, 1914
Lawrence T. Allen   7,879   51
Charles G. Taylor   7,210   46
George W. Berry   451   3

November 5, 1918
Thomas A. Graham   8,057   64
W. O. Edwards   4,459   36

November 7, 1922
Thomas A. Graham, R   12,068   59
Owen M. Burns, D   8,072   40
Fred Witt, S   291   1

April 7, 1925
William T. Henderson, R   10,248   54
Andrew B. Dennis, D   8,641   46

November 2, 1926
William T. Henderson, R   14,872   100

November 4, 1930
Harlin M. Steely, R   12,765   56
Everett L. Dalbey, D   10,231   44

November 6, 1934
Harlin M. Steely, R   18,354   54
Andrew B. Dennis, D   15,850   46

November 8, 1938
Harlin M. Steely, R   21,269   57
Thomas C. Stifler, D   15,972   43

November 3, 1942
Harlin M. Steely, R   18,605   65
Henry S. Wise, D   10,207   35

November 5, 1946
Harlin M. Steely, R   19,815   63
Henry S. Wise, D   11,651   37

November 7, 1950
Frank J. Meyer, R   22,398   62
Wayne Cook, D   13,663   38

November 2, 1954
Frank J. Meyer, R   20,179   58
Ray M. Foreman, D   14,601   42

November 4, 1958
Frank J. Meyer, R   17,234   51
John A. Lambright, D   16,249   49

James R. Glenn

November 6, 1962
James K. Robinson, R   19,920   54
John A. Lambright, D   16,643   46

PROBATE JUDGE
November 8, 1910
Clinton Abernathy   8,032   64
W. O. Edwards   3,429   28
William L. Campbell   621   5
Isaac Elsdon   387   3

November 3, 1914
Walter J. Bookwalter   8,037   67
James C. Woodbury   3,518   29
Thomas Scopes   483   4

November 5, 1918
Walter J. Bookwalter   7,558   62
Everett L. Dalbey   4,667   38

November 7, 1922
Walter J. Bookwalter, R   11,354   58
Samuel V. Jinkins, D   8,291   42

November 2, 1926
Walter J. Bookwalter, R   14,744   100

November 4, 1930 *
Walter J. Bookwalter, R   11,701   50
Ralph M. Jinkins, D   11,518   50

November 6, 1934
Ralph M. Jinkins, D   18,009   54
John W. Speakman, R   15,210   46

November 8, 1938
Arthur R. Hall, R   18,841   52
Ralph M. Jinkins, D   17,730   48

November 3, 1942
Arthur R. Hall, R   18,045   64
Ralph M. Jinkins, D   10,205   36

November 5, 1946
Arthur R. Hall, R   20,028   65
Nelson M. Willis, D   10,721   35

November 7, 1950
Arthur R. Hall, R   23,319   100

November 2, 1954
John W. Unger, R   17,743   60
Henry S. Wise, D   11,845   40

November 4, 1958
Paul M. Wright, D   18,385   55
Lawrence T. Allen, Jr., R   14,812   45

November 6, 1962
Paul M. Wright, D   20,040   55
Albert Saikley, R   16,538   45

CIRCUIT JUDGE
November 8, 1988 - Robinson Vacancy
Thomas J. Fahey, D   17,441   51
Jerry A. Davis, R   16,801   49

November 8, 1988 - Wright Vacancy
John P. O'Rourke, D   19,845   57
Thomas B. Meyer, R   14,673   43

November 3, 1998
Michael D. Clary, D   11,884   50
Charles C. Hall, R   11,871   50

November 7, 2000 - O'Rourke Vacancy
Craig H. DeArmond, R   16,268   51
David J. Ryan, D   15,538   49

November 7, 2006 - Fahey Vacancy
Nancy S. Fahey, D   11,606   51
Frank R. Young, R   11,302   49

STATE'S ATTORNEY
November 5, 1872
Peter Walsh   2,965   58
William D. Lindsey   2,154   42

November 7, 1876
Joseph W. Jones   3,931   53
William D. Lindsey   3,431   47

November 2, 1880
James A. Outland   5,134   58
John M. Davis   3,673   42

<table>
<tr><td colspan="3"><u>April 5, 1881</u></td><td colspan="3"><u>November 2, 1920</u></td></tr>
<tr><td>Charles M. Swallow</td><td>3,439</td><td>66</td><td>John H. Lewman, R</td><td>17,777</td><td>66</td></tr>
<tr><td>George W. Salmans</td><td>1,780</td><td>34</td><td>Oliver D. Mann, D</td><td>8,984</td><td>34</td></tr>
<tr><td colspan="3"><u>November 4, 1884</u></td><td colspan="3"><u>November 4, 1924</u></td></tr>
<tr><td>William J. Calhoun</td><td>5,760</td><td>58</td><td>Elmer O. Furrow, R</td><td>19,174</td><td>65</td></tr>
<tr><td>George R. Tilton</td><td>4,099</td><td>42</td><td>Ralph Rouse, D</td><td>10,444</td><td>35</td></tr>
<tr><td colspan="3"><u>November 6, 1888</u></td><td colspan="3"><u>November 6, 1928</u></td></tr>
<tr><td>Hiram P. Blackburn</td><td>6,252</td><td>56</td><td>Elmer O. Furrow, R</td><td>21,986</td><td>67</td></tr>
<tr><td>Joseph B. Mann</td><td>4,586</td><td>41</td><td>Jack N. Moore, D</td><td>10,753</td><td>33</td></tr>
<tr><td>David N. Campbell</td><td>309</td><td>3</td><td colspan="3"><u>November 8, 1932</u></td></tr>
<tr><td>Jesse Harper</td><td>95</td><td>1</td><td>Oliver D. Mann, D</td><td>21,714</td><td>56</td></tr>
<tr><td colspan="3"><u>November 8, 1892</u></td><td>Elmer O. Furrow, R</td><td>16,910</td><td>44</td></tr>
<tr><td>Seymour G. Wilson</td><td>6,878</td><td>57</td><td></td><td></td><td></td></tr>
<tr><td>James A. Meeks</td><td>5,039</td><td>42</td><td colspan="3"><u>November 3, 1936</u></td></tr>
<tr><td>George W. Smith</td><td>156</td><td>1</td><td>Oliver D. Mann, D</td><td>23,192</td><td>55</td></tr>
<tr><td></td><td></td><td></td><td>David Allison, R</td><td>18,854</td><td>45</td></tr>
<tr><td colspan="3"><u>November 3, 1896</u></td><td></td><td></td><td></td></tr>
<tr><td>Seymour G. Wilson</td><td>8,749</td><td>60</td><td colspan="3"><u>November 5, 1940</u></td></tr>
<tr><td>A. C. Rudolph</td><td>5,780</td><td>40</td><td>William T. Henderson, R</td><td>22,174</td><td>51</td></tr>
<tr><td></td><td></td><td></td><td>Oliver D. Mann, D</td><td>21,539</td><td>49</td></tr>
<tr><td colspan="3"><u>November 6, 1900</u></td><td></td><td></td><td></td></tr>
<tr><td>John W. Keeslar</td><td>9,796</td><td>62</td><td colspan="3"><u>November 7, 1944</u></td></tr>
<tr><td>Andrew B. Dennis</td><td>6,041</td><td>38</td><td>William T. Henderson, R</td><td>20,016</td><td>54</td></tr>
<tr><td></td><td></td><td></td><td>Oliver D. Mann, D</td><td>16,997</td><td>46</td></tr>
<tr><td colspan="3"><u>November 8, 1904</u></td><td></td><td></td><td></td></tr>
<tr><td>John W. Keeslar</td><td>10,927</td><td>69</td><td colspan="3"><u>November 2, 1948</u></td></tr>
<tr><td>Andrew B. Dennis</td><td>3,773</td><td>24</td><td>William T. Henderson, R</td><td>17,641</td><td>52</td></tr>
<tr><td>Charles E. Brown</td><td>1,126</td><td>7</td><td>Henry S. Wise, D</td><td>16,204</td><td>48</td></tr>
<tr><td colspan="3"><u>November 3, 1908</u></td><td colspan="3"><u>November 4, 1952</u></td></tr>
<tr><td>John H. Lewman</td><td>10,957</td><td>60</td><td>John T. Allen, R</td><td>23,457</td><td>56</td></tr>
<tr><td>Charles G. Taylor</td><td>7,338</td><td>40</td><td>Paul M. Wright, D</td><td>18,474</td><td>44</td></tr>
<tr><td colspan="3"><u>November 5, 1912</u></td><td colspan="3"><u>November 6, 1956</u></td></tr>
<tr><td>John H. Lewman</td><td>6,823</td><td>39</td><td>John R. Dean, R</td><td>22,337</td><td>52</td></tr>
<tr><td>Oliver D. Mann</td><td>5,882</td><td>34</td><td>Kenneth H. Clapper, D</td><td>20,369</td><td>48</td></tr>
<tr><td>George G. Mabin</td><td>3,565</td><td>20</td><td></td><td></td><td></td></tr>
<tr><td>O. P. Brown</td><td>684</td><td>4</td><td colspan="3"><u>November 8, 1960</u></td></tr>
<tr><td>Arthur Allison</td><td>546</td><td>3</td><td>John R. Dean, R</td><td>23,518</td><td>52</td></tr>
<tr><td></td><td></td><td></td><td>Gino Groppi, D</td><td>21,483</td><td>48</td></tr>
<tr><td colspan="3"><u>November 7, 1916</u></td><td></td><td></td><td></td></tr>
<tr><td>John H. Lewman</td><td>10,385</td><td>54</td><td colspan="3"><u>November 3, 1964</u></td></tr>
<tr><td>Oliver D. Mann</td><td>8,953</td><td>46</td><td>John P. O'Rourke, D</td><td>22,634</td><td>53</td></tr>
<tr><td></td><td></td><td></td><td>John W. Unger, R</td><td>20,017</td><td>47</td></tr>
</table>

November 5, 1968
John Morton Jones, R 22,969 56
Raymond F. Rose, D 17,892 44

November 3, 1970
John W. Unger, R 20,084 100

November 7, 1972
Richard J. Doyle, D 20,321 52
Everett L. Laury, R 18,562 48

November 2, 1976
Thomas J. Fahey, D 19,149 52
Edward Litak, R 17,770 48

November 4, 1980
Edward Litak, R 19,851 52
Thomas J. Fahey, D 18,356 48

November 6, 1984
Craig H. DeArmond, R 22,033 59
Charles J. Devens, D 15,569 41

November 8, 1988
Craig H. DeArmond, R 18,952 55
Michael D. Clary, D 15,703 45

November 3, 1992
Michael D. Clary, D 19,329 52
Craig H. DeArmond, R 18,170 48

November 5, 1996
Michael D. Clary, D 19,200 64
Randy A. Lakey, R 10,954 36

November 7, 2000
Frank R. Young, R 16,370 52
Paul T. Manion, D 15,076 48

November 2, 2004
Frank R. Young, R 19,565 60
William T. Donahue, D 13,208 40

November 4, 2008
Randall J. Brinegar, R 15,934 51
Daniel D. Brown, D 15,539 49

* Result changed by election contest
D - Democratic   S - Socialist
R - Republican

CONTESTED PRIMARY ELECTIONS
(Since 1930)
COUNTY JUDGE
April 8, 1930 - Republican
Harlin M. Steely 11,773 57
William T. Henderson 8,802 43

April 10, 1934 - Republican
Harlin M. Steely 11,344 72
Elmer O. Furrow 4,382 28

April 14, 1942 - Republican
Harlin M. Steely 10,343 62
John R. Dean 6,287 38

April 11, 1950 - Republican
Frank J. Meyer 8,598 48
Thomas A. Graham 6,751 38
John R. Dean 2,521 14

April 10, 1962 - Democratic
John A. Lambright 5,966 73
Samuel M. McKendree 2,152 27

PROBATE JUDGE
April 8, 1930 - Republican
Walter J. Bookwalter 9,922 53
W. R. Jewell 8,862 47

April 10, 1934 - Republican
John W. Speakman 6,268 47
Wilbur R. Wicks 5,873 44
E. L. McDuffee 1,298 10

April 12, 1938 - Democratic
Ralph M. Jinkins 8,653 81
Nathan Odle 2,050 19

April 12, 1938 - Republican
Arthur R. Hall 6,215 63
John R. Dean 3,728 37

April 9, 1946 - Democratic
Nelson M. Willis	77	51
Oliver D. Mann	73	49

April 9, 1946 - Republican
Arthur R. Hall	6,101	55
John W. Unger	5,050	45

April 11, 1950 - Republican
Arthur R. Hall	7,656	46
Ben Norwood	5,734	34
Harold A. Craig	3,375	20

April 13, 1954 - Republican
John W. Unger	5,694	40
Ben Norwood	4,959	35
Harold A. Craig	3,616	25

April 8, 1958 - Republican
Lawrence T. Allen, Jr.	8,063	55
John W. Unger	6,729	45

April 10, 1962 - Republican
Albert Saikley	7,066	54
John W. Unger	6,006	46

CIRCUIT JUDGE
March 15, 1988 - Democratic
Thomas J. Fahey	3,555	64
Marion Eugene Wright	1,981	36

March 15, 1988 - Republican
Jerry A. Davis	4,904	76
Theodore Pasierb	1,550	24

March 17, 1998 - Republican
Charles C. Hall	2,917	45
Christopher P. Meyer	2,742	42
Robert E. McIntire	797	12

March 21, 2006 - Democratic
Nancy S. Fahey	1,402	56
Daniel D. Brown	1,106	44

STATE'S ATTORNEY
April 12, 1932 - Democratic
Oliver D. Mann	2,434	51
Samuel V. Jinkins	2,303	49

April 12, 1932 - Republican
Elmer O. Furrow	9,193	49
David Allison	8,668	46
Eldon L. McLaughlin	869	5

April 14, 1936 - Republican
David Allison	3,632	27
Leo W. Burk	3,444	26
Elmer O. Furrow	3,249	24
H. Ernest Hutton	3,100	23

April 9, 1940 - Republican
William T. Henderson	5,592	36
Elmer O. Furrow	4,965	32
John R. Dean	2,573	17
H. J. Hasch	2,260	15

April 10, 1956 - Republican
John R. Dean	3,096	59
David Allison	2,114	41

April 14, 1964 - Republican
John W. Unger	8,443	61
John R. Dean	5,376	39

March 16, 1976 - Democratic
Thomas J. Fahey	5,720	65
Richard E. Server	3,125	35

March 16, 1976 - Republican
Edward Litak	4,203	56
John R. McClory	3,336	44

March 17, 1992 - Democratic
Michael D. Clary	4,557	60
Larry S. Mills	3,089	40

March 21, 2000 - Democratic
Paul T. Manion	3,436	61
Larry S. Mills	2,163	39

February 5, 2008 - Democratic
Daniel D. Brown	2,996	41
William T. Donahue	2,458	33
Derek J. Girton	1,923	26

James R. Glenn

SOURCES
Abstract of Election Returns 1818-1850, 605; Abstract of Election Returns 1850-1862, 195, 233, 310; Abstract of Election Returns 1862-1873, 35, 126, 277, 445; Abstract of Election Returns 1873-1882, 40, 159, 195, 332, 343; Abstract of Election Returns 1882-1912, 46, 87, 141, 196, 259, 298, 353, 394, 401, 445, 488, 540, 580, 23, 44, 46, 66, 67, 86, 112, 133, 157, 175, 199, 216, 219, 239, 256, 279, 298, 319, 333, 355; Abstract of Votes for County Officers Cast in the County of Vermilion and State of Illinois, at the Election Held in said County, on 11/8/1853, 4/10/1934, 4/12/1938, 11/5/1940, 11/3/1942, 11/7/1944, 11/5/1946, 11/2/1948, 11/7/1950, 11/4/1952, 11/2/1954, 11/6/1956, 11/4/1958, 11/8/1960, 11/5/1968; State of Illinois Official Vote Cast at the General Election 1988, 115-116; 1998, 126-127; 2000, 95-96; 2006, 136; Danville Commercial-News 4/9/30, 5, 4/17/32, Sec. 2, 6, 4/16/36, 10, 4/14/40, 5, 4/15/42,1, 4/16/42, Sec. 2, 1, 4/10/46, 1, 4/11/46, Sec. 2, 1, 4/12/50, 1, 4/14/50, 13, 4/14/54, 13, 4/18/54, 11, 4/11/56, 15, 4/12/56, 21, 4/10/58, 21, 4/15/62, 21, 11/11/62, 21, 4/19/64, 23, 34, 11/4/64, 15, 11/6/64, 11, 11/6/68, 23, 11/7/70, 3; State of Illinois Official Vote Cast at the General Primary Election 1988, 237-238; 1998, 149; www.elections.state.il.us, 3/21/06; Records of Vermilion County Clerk, Lynn Foster and staff (2010).

HIGHER COURTS (local candidates)
SUPREME COURT
June 2, 1873 - Thornton Vacancy
* John Scholfield	16,607	60
Arius A. Kingsbury	10,915	40

June 2, 1879
* John Scholfield	27,446	100

June 4, 1888
* John Scholfield	14,130	100

June 4, 1888 - Scott Vacancy
* Jacob W. Wilkin	23,425	100

June 7, 1897
* Jacob W. Wilkin, R	48,772	55
William E. Nelson, D	39,190	45

June 4, 1906
* Jacob W. Wilkin, R	20,239	88
J. T. Jones, S	2,637	12

June 8, 1907 - Wilkin Vacancy
* Frank K. Dunn, R	34,115	59
James A. Creighton, D	24,027	41

June 7, 1915
* Frank K. Dunn, R	36,647	59
Louis Fitzhenry, D	32,781	53

June 2, 1924
* Frank K. Dunn, R	26,094	60
Lawrence B. Stringer, D	17,479	40

June 27, 1938 - Herrick Vacancy
* Walter T. Gunn, R	80,592	55
Joseph L. McLaughlin, D	66,525	45

June 1, 1942
* Walter T. Gunn, R	14,208	100

June 4, 1951 - Gunn Vacancy
* George W. Bristow, R	57,824	63
Charles M. Webber, D	34,621	37

June 6, 1960
* George W. Bristow, R	3,558	100

April 10, 1962 - Bristow Vacancy
Robert C. Underwood, R	117,600	60
* Robert Z. Hickman, D	79,011	40

November 5, 2002 - Miller Vacancy
* Rita B. Garman, R	225,693	53
Sue E. Myerscough, D	198,500	47

APPELLATE COURT
November 3, 1964
Samuel O. Smith, R	251,164	17
Harold F. Trapp, D	251,010	17
James C. Craven, D	249,926	17

Stanley Thomas, R   249,279   17
Fred W. Reither, D   247,012   17
* Albert Saikley, R   241,382   16

November 2, 1976 - Smith Vacancy
Richard Mills, R   233,710   52
* Paul M. Wright, D   217,072   48

November 4, 1986 - Mills Vacancy
* Carl A. Lund, R   274,227   100

November 5, 1996 - Lund Vacancy
* Rita B. Garman, R   352,847   100

D - Democrat   S - Socialist
R - Republican

CONTESTED PRIMARY ELECTIONS (Since 1964)
SUPREME COURT
March 19, 2002 - Republican
* Rita B. Garman   94,155   63
Robert J. Steigmann   54,278   37

APPELLATE COURT
March 19, 1974 - Democratic
Robert W. McCarthy   30,760   40
* Paul M. Wright   18,332   24
Harold A. Baker   15,838   21
Thomas F. Walsh   11,929   16

March 19, 1974 - Republican
Frederick S. Green   40,528   50
Richard Mills   31,610   39
* Albert Saikley   8,180   10

March 20, 1984 - Republican
John T. McCullough   26,979   61
* Carl A. Lund   17,394   39

March 18, 1986 - Republican
* Carl A. Lund   54,141   57
Frank M. Brady   40,930   43

* Candidate from Clark, Coles, Cumberland, Edgar, or Vermilion County

SOURCES
Abstract of Election Returns 1873-1882, 10, 247; *Abstract of Election Returns 1882-1912*, 116, 117, 475; *State of Illinois Official Vote Cast at the General Election 1898*, 48; *1906*, 52; *1915*, 51; *1938*, 42; *1942*, 36; *1952*, 56; *1960*, 59; *1962*, 53; *1964*, 148; *1976*, 74; *1986*, 103; *1996*, 100; *2002*, 131; *Blue Book of the State of Illinois, 1925-1926*, 679-680, 864; *State of Illinois Official Vote Cast at the General Primary Election 1974*, 113; *1984*, 152; *1986*, 101; *2002*, 144-145.

CIRCUIT JUDGE RETENTION

	Yes	*No*	*Pct.*
November 3, 1964			
R. Cotton	61,631	9,172	87.05
J. Spivey	59,705	9,322	86.50
H. Hannah	59,464	9,316	86.45
November 8, 1966			
Clark			
Z. Arbogast	4,633	2,150	68.30
Coles			
J. Berkowitz	11,388	1,812	86.27
W. Sunderman	12,082	1,795	87.06
Edgar			
H. Ruff	6,763	2,506	72.96
Vermilion			
P. Wright	22,512	4,879	82.19
J. Robinson	22,088	5,267	80.75
November 3, 1970			
R. Cotton	44,575	11,900	78.93
J. Spivey	43,354	11,522	79.00
H. Hannah	42,894	12,537	77.38
November 7, 1972			
J. Berkowitz	44,265	11,900	78.81
W. Sunderman	43,954	11,172	79.73
P. Wright	47,200	10,955	81.16
J. Robinson	47,208	11,272	80.73
J. Watson	42,588	10,857	79.69
C. Bennett	42,858	10,884	79.75

<u>November 7, 1978</u>
W. Sunderman	29,428	7,874	78.89
P. Wright	31,104	8,005	79.53
J. Robinson	30,757	8,009	79.34
J. Watson	27,350	8,183	76.97
C. Bennett	27,507	8,066	77.33

<u>November 4, 1980</u>
R. Pearman	38,298	11,952	76.21
C. Lund	36,286	12,720	74.04

<u>November 6, 1984</u>
W. Sunderman	43,551	11,519	79.08
P. Wright	43,127	10,975	79.71
J. Robinson	40,237	13,503	74.87
J. Watson	38,820	10,940	78.01
C. Bennett	41,621	11,583	78.23
J. Spitz	42,259	11,472	78.65

<u>November 4, 1986</u>
R. Pearman	32,154	8,591	78.92
C. Lund	31,891	8,518	78.92
P. Komada	28,737	11,943	70.64

<u>November 6, 1990</u>
J. Spitz	32,176	11,850	73.08

<u>November 3, 1992</u>
R. Pearman	46,084	11,981	79.37
P. Komada	44,504	13,894	76.21
R. Garman	48,936	10,779	81.95

<u>November 8, 1994</u>
R. Scott	29,232	8,762	76.94
J. O'Rourke	29,777	8,537	77.72
T. Fahey	28,889	9,318	75.61

<u>November 5, 1996</u>
A. Waller	37,023	10,361	78.13
R. Cochonour	35,278	10,705	76.72
T. Resch	36,269	10,212	78.03

<u>November 3, 1998</u>
P. Komada	36,989	11,187	76.78
G. Jacobs	36,547	10,185	78.21

<u>November 7, 2000</u>
T. Fahey	48,949	13,102	78.89

<u>November 5, 2002</u>
A. Waller	36,944	9,571	79.42
T. Resch	37,122	9,218	80.11
D. Cini	36,453	9,924	78.60

<u>November 2, 2004</u>
G. Jacobs	51,686	10,232	83.47
C. Anderson	51,755	10,835	82.69
M. Clary	50,483	11,350	81.64
J. Glenn	51,098	10,275	83.26

<u>November 7, 2006</u>
C. DeArmond	37,653	9,531	79.80

<u>November 4, 2008</u>
T. Resch	55,736	12,155	82.10
M. Shick	54,319	13,405	80.21

<u>November 2, 2010</u>
G. Jacobs	38,539	10,170	79.12
C. Anderson	37,206	12,015	75.59
M. Clary	36,600	12,187	75.02
J. Glenn	38,085	9,888	79.39
M. Everhart	37,122	10,626	77.75
T. Righter	38,868	9,868	79.75

SOURCES

State of Illinois Official Vote Cast at the General Election 1964, 140; *1966*, 54-56; *1970*, 59; *1972*, 78; *1978*, 92-93; *1980*, 75; *1984*, 81; *1986*, 127-128; *1990*, 148; *1992*, 184-185; *1994*, 175-176; *1996*, 159-160; *1998*, 176; *2000*, 120; *2002*, 181-182; *2004*, 145-146; *2006*, 164; <u>www.elections.state.il.us</u>, 11/4/08, 11/2/10; <u>www.co.vermilion.il.us/cntyclrk/results-1.htm</u>; <u>www.co.vermilion.il.us/el45a.htm</u>.

ROSTERS

CIRCUIT JUDGES (1819-1897)
CLARK COUNTY
Second Circuit

1819-1820	Thomas C. Browne (S.Ct.)
1820-1824	William Wilson (S.Ct.)

Fifth Circuit

1825-1827	James O. Wattles

Fourth Circuit

1827-1835	William Wilson (S.Ct.)
1835-1841	Justin Harlan
1841-1848	William Wilson (S.Ct.)
1848-1861	Justin Harlan
1861-1865	Charles H. Constable
1865-1873	Hiram B. Decius

Fifteenth Circuit

1873-1877	Oliver L. Davis

Fourth Circuit (three positions)

1877-1879	William E. Nelson, *Decatur*
1877-1885	Oliver L. Davis, *Danville*
1877-1891	Charles B. Smith, *Champaign*
1879-1888	Jacob W. Wilkin, *Marshall*
1885-1891	James F. Hughes, *Mattoon*
1888-1897	Edward P. Vail, *Decatur*
1891-1897	Francis M. Wright, *Urbana*
1891-1897	Ferdinand Bookwalter, *Danville*

COLES COUNTY
Fourth Circuit

1830-1835	William Wilson (S.Ct.)
1835-1841	Justin Harlan
1841-1848	William Wilson (S.Ct.)
1848-1857	Justin Harlan

Seventeenth Circuit

1857-1859	Charles Emmerson

Fourth Circuit

1859-1861	Justin Harlan
1861-1865	Charles H. Constable

Twenty-Seventh Circuit

1865-1866	Oliver L. Davis
1866-1873	James Steele

Fifteenth Circuit

1873-1877	Oliver L. Davis

Fourth Circuit (three positions)

1877-1879	William E. Nelson, *Decatur*
1877-1885	Oliver L. Davis, *Danville*
1877-1891	Charles B. Smith, *Champaign*
1879-1888	Jacob W. Wilkin, *Marshall*
1885-1891	James F. Hughes, *Mattoon*
1888-1897	Edward P. Vail, *Decatur*
1891-1897	Francis M. Wright, *Urbana*
1891-1897	Ferdinand Bookwalter, *Danville*

CUMBERLAND COUNTY
Fourth Circuit

1843-1848	William Wilson (S.Ct.)
1848-1861	Justin Harlan
1861-1865	Charles H. Constable
1865-1873	Hiram B. Decius

Twenty-First Circuit

1873-1877	James C. Allen

Second Circuit (three positions)

1877-1879	John H. Halley, *Newton*
1877-1879	James C. Allen, *Palestine*
1877-1879	Tazewell B. Tanner, *Mt. Vernon*
1879-1885	Thomas S. Casey, *Mt. Vernon*
1879-1891	Chauncey S. Conger, *Carmi*
1879-1891	William C. Jones, *Robinson*
1885-1897	Carroll C. Boggs, *Fairfield*
1891-1897	Silas Z. Landes, *Mt. Carmel*
1891-1897	Edmund D. Youngblood, *Shawneetown*

EDGAR COUNTY
Second Circuit

1823-1824	William Wilson (S.Ct.)

Fifth Circuit

1825-1827	James O. Wattles

Fourth Circuit

1827-1835	William Wilson (S.Ct.)
1835-1841	Justin Harlan
1841-1845	William Wilson (S.Ct.)

Eighth Circuit

1845-1848	Samuel H. Treat (S.Ct.)
1848-1853	David Davis

Fourth Circuit

1853-1861	Justin Harlan
1861-1865	Charles H. Constable

Twenty-Seventh Circuit

1865-1866	Oliver L. Davis
1866-1873	James Steele

Fifteenth Circuit

1873-1877	Oliver L. Davis

Fourth Circuit (three positions)

1877-1879	William E. Nelson, *Decatur*
1877-1885	Oliver L. Davis, *Danville*
1877-1891	Charles B. Smith, *Champaign*
1879-1888	Jacob W. Wilkin, *Marshall*
1885-1891	James F. Hughes, *Mattoon*
1888-1897	Edward P. Vail, *Decatur*
1891-1897	Francis M. Wright, *Urbana*
1891-1897	Ferdinand Bookwalter, *Danville*

VERMILION COUNTY

Fifth Circuit

1826-1827	James O. Wattles

Fourth Circuit

1827-1835	William Wilson (S.Ct.)
1835-1841	Justin Harlan
1841-1845	William Wilson (S.Ct.)

Eighth Circuit

1845-1848	Samuel H. Treat (S.Ct.)
1848-1861	David Davis

Twenty-Seventh Circuit

1861-1866	Oliver L. Davis
1866-1873	James Steele

Fifteenth Circuit

1873-1877	Oliver L. Davis

Fourth Circuit (three positions)

1877-1879	William E. Nelson, *Decatur*
1877-1885	Oliver L. Davis, *Danville*
1877-1891	Charles B. Smith, *Champaign*
1879-1888	Jacob W. Wilkin, *Marshall*
1885-1891	James F. Hughes, *Mattoon*
1888-1897	Edward P. Vail, *Decatur*
1891-1897	Francis M. Wright, *Urbana*
1891-1897	Ferdinand Bookwalter, *Danville*

STATE'S ATTORNEYS
(1819-1872)
CLARK COUNTY

Second Circuit

1819-1824	John M. Robinson

Fifth Circuit

1824-1827	John M. Robinson

Fourth Circuit

1827-1830	John M. Robinson
1831-1835	Edwin B. Webb
1835-1836	Orlando B. Ficklin
1836-1837	Aaron Shaw
1837-1839	Augustus C. French
1839-1841	Garland B. Shelledy
1841-1843	Aaron Shaw
1843-1856	Alfred Kitchell
1856-1860	John Scholfield
1860-1864	James R. Cunningham
1864-1872	Silas S. Whitehead

COLES COUNTY

Fourth Circuit

1831-1835	Edwin B. Webb
1835-1836	Orlando B. Ficklin
1836-1837	Aaron Shaw
1837-1839	Augustus C. French
1839-1841	Garland B. Shelledy
1841-1843	Aaron Shaw
1843-1856	Alfred Kitchell
1856-1857	John Scholfield

Seventeenth Circuit

1857-1859	John R. Eden

Fourth Circuit

1859-1860	John Scholfield
1860-1864	James R. Cunningham
1864-1865	Silas S. Whitehead

Twenty-Seventh Circuit

1865-1868	Joseph G. Cannon
1868-1870	John Boyle
1870-1872	Alexander P. Dunbar

CUMBERLAND COUNTY

Fourth Circuit

1843-1856	Alfred Kitchell
1856-1860	John Scholfield
1860-1864	James R. Cunningham
1864-1872	Silas S. Whitehead

EDGAR COUNTY

Second Circuit

1823-1824	John M. Robinson

Fifth Circuit

1824-1827	John M. Robinson

Fourth Circuit

1827-1830	John M. Robinson
1831-1835	Edwin B. Webb
1835-1836	Orlando B. Ficklin
1836-1837	Aaron Shaw
1837-1839	Augustus C. French
1839-1841	Garland B. Shelledy
1841-1843	Aaron Shaw
1843-1845	Alfred Kitchell

Eighth Circuit

1845-1846	James A. McDougall
1846-1853	David B. Campbell

Fourth Circuit

1853-1856	Alfred Kitchell
1856-1860	John Scholfield
1860-1864	James R. Cunningham
1864-1865	Silas S. Whitehead

Twenty-Seventh Circuit

1865-1868	Joseph G. Cannon
1868-1870	John Boyle
1870-1872	Alexander P. Dunbar

VERMILION COUNTY

Fifth Circuit

1826-1827	John M. Robinson

Fourth Circuit

1827-1830	John M. Robinson
1831-1835	Edwin B. Webb
1835-1836	Orlando B. Ficklin
1836-1837	Aaron Shaw
1837-1839	Augustus C. French
1839-1841	Garland B. Shelledy
1841-1843	Aaron Shaw
1843-1845	Alfred Kitchell

Eighth Circuit

1845-1846	James A. McDougall
1846-1856	David B. Campbell
1856-1861	Ward H. Lamon

Twenty-Seventh Circuit

1861-1868	Joseph G. Cannon
1868-1870	John Boyle
1870-1872	Alexander P. Dunbar

CIRCUIT JUDGES (1897-   )

Fifth Circuit (three positions)

1897-1902	Ferdinand Bookwalter, *Danville*
1897-1903	Henry Van Sellar, *Paris*
1897-1903	Frank K. Dunn, *Charleston*
1902-1915	Morton W. Thompson, *Danville*
1903-1909	James W. Craig, *Mattoon*
1903-1915	E. R. E. Kimbrough, *Danville*
1909-1915	William B. Scholfield, *Marshall*
1915-1927	Augustus A. Partlow, *Danville*
1915-1927	Walter Brewer, *Toledo*
1915-1927	John H. Marshall, *Charleston*
1927-1933	S. Murray Clark, *Danville*
1927-1951	George W. Bristow, *Paris*
1927-1933	Charles A. Shuey, *Charleston*
1933-1935	Craig Van Meter, *Mattoon*
1933-1949	Casper S. Platt, *Danville*
1936-1939	Grendel F. Bennett, *Marshall*
1939-1957	Ben F. Anderson, *Charleston*
1951-1963	John F. Spivey, *Danville*
1951-1963	Robert F. Cotton, *Paris*
1957-1963	Harry I. Hannah, *Mattoon*

Spivey Judgeship

1964-1971	John F. Spivey, *Danville*
1971-1979	Frank J. Meyer, *Danville*
1980-1985	John P. Meyer, *Danville*
1986	Matthew A. Jurczak, *Danville*
1986-1996	Rita B. Garman, *Danville*
1997-	Claudia S. Anderson, *Danville*

Cotton Judgeship

1964-1971	Robert F. Cotton, *Paris*
1972-1998	Ralph S. Pearman, *Paris*
1998-	James R. Glenn, *Mattoon*

Hannah Judgeship

1964-1973	Harry I. Hannah, *Mattoon*
1973-1980	Thomas M. Burke, *Charleston*
1980-2001	Paul C. Komada, *Charleston*
2001-	Mitchell K. Shick, *Charleston*

James R. Glenn

Cini Judgeship
1996-2008   Dale A. Cini, *Mattoon*
2008-2010   Richard E. Scott, *Paris*
             (recalled)
2010-   Matthew L. Sullivan, *Paris*

CLARK COUNTY
JUDGES
Judges of Probate
1821-1823   Samuel Prevo
1823-1825   Charles Neeley
1825-1835   Jacob Harlan
1835-1837   Uri Manley
Probate Justices of the Peace
1837-1843   Uri Manley
1843-1849   Stephen Archer
County Judges
1849-1853   Stephen Archer
1853-1854   John Bartlett
1854-1857   John Stockwell
1857-1869   William C. Whitlock
1869-1873   William R. Griffith
1873-1877   Justin Harlan
1877-1882   William R. Griffith
1882-1886   Ethan A. Sutton
1886-1894   Henry Gasaway
1894-1898   William T. Hollenbeck
1898-1902   J. C. Perdue
1902-1906   Everett Connelly
1906-1914   Hershel R. Snavely
1914-1918   A. L. Ruffner
1918-1922   Edward Pearce
1922-1926   Harry M. Janney
1926-1932   Jed Gard
1934-1938   C. A. Williams
1938-1946   Theodore Thompson
1946-1958   John M. Hollenbeck
1958-1963   Zollie O. Arbogast
Associate Judges
1964-1967   Zollie O. Arbogast
1968-1971   Caslon K. Bennett
Circuit Judges
1971-1988   Caslon K. Bennett

1988-1989   Zollie O. Arbogast
1990   James K. Robinson (recalled)
1990-   Tracy W. Resch

STATE'S ATTORNEYS
1872-1876   John L. Ryan
1876-1884   Thomas L. Orndorff
1884-1888   Newton Tibbs
1888-1896   Thomas L. Orndorff
1896-1900   Samuel M. Scholfield
1900-1904   M. B. Davison
1904-1908   Arthur Poorman
1908-1912   Everett Connelly
1912-1916   Edmund D. Jones
1916-1920   Olen R. Clements
1920-1928   Everett Connelly
1928-1932   Victor C. Miller
1932-1936   Carson M. Purdunn
1936-1940   John M. Hollenbeck
1940-1952   Claude W. McDaniel
1952-1956   William H. Downey
1956-1976   Omer T. Shawler
1976-1981   Tracy W. Resch
1981-2001   David W. Lewis
2001-   Dennis E. Simonton

COLES COUNTY
JUDGES
Judges of Probate
1831-1834   James P. Jones
1834   John F. Smyth
1834-1835   S. M. Dunbar
1835-1837   William Collom
Probate Justices of the Peace
1837-1841   Reuben Canterbury
1841-1843   John W. Trower
1843-1847   Robert S. Mills
1847-1849   William W. Bishop
County Judges
1849-1857   William W. Bishop
1857-1864   Gideon Edwards
1864-1865   Joshua P. Cooper
1865-1869   McHenry Brooks
1869-1873   Abner M. Peterson

1873-1877	William E. Adams
1877-1882	James R. Cunningham
1882-1886	Charles Bennett
1886-1894	Lapsley C. Henley
1894-1898	Sumner S. Anderson
1898-1902	John P. Harrah
1902-1910	T. N. Cofer
1910-1922	John P. Harrah
1922-1930	J. B. Lane
1930-1950	John T. Kincaid
1950-1963	William J. Sunderman

Associate Judges

1964-1971	William J. Sunderman

Circuit Judges

1971-1989	William J. Sunderman
1989-2003	Ashton C. Waller
2004-	Teresa K. Righter

Justices of the Common Pleas Court-Mattoon

1869	William W. Craddock
1869-1872	Charles B. Steele
1872-1873	Horace S. Clark

City Judges-Mattoon

1898-1902	James F. Hughes
1902-1906	Lapsley C. Henley
1906-1907	Horace S. Clark
1909-1910	George D. Wilson
1910-1922	John C. McNutt
1922-1925	Isaac B. Craig
1925-1936	Clarence H. Douglas
1936-1963	Jacob Berkowitz

Associate Judges

1964-1971	Jacob Berkowitz

Circuit Judges

1971-1976	Jacob Berkowitz
1977-1991	Joseph R. Spitz
1992-2011	Gary W. Jacobs

City Judges-Charleston

1910-1914	Charles A. Shuey
1914-1918	Charles A. Quackenbush
1918-1922	John T. Kincaid

1922-1930	Ben F. Anderson
1930-1936	Herbert S. Anderson
1936-1960	C. Wade Barrick
1960-1962	Jack H. Anderson

STATE'S ATTORNEYS

1872-1876	James W. Craig
1876-1880	Robert M. Gray
1880-1888	Samuel M. Leitch
1888-1896	John H. Marshall
1896-1900	Emery Andrews
1900-1904	John F. Voigt
1904-1908	John C. McNutt
1908-1916	Robert G. Hammond
1916-1920	Emery Andrews
1920-1928	Charles H. Fletcher
1928-1932	C. M. Heinlein
1932-1940	Jewell I. Dilsaver
1940-1948	William K. Kidwell
1948-1956	Hugh Harwood
1956-1960	Thomas M. Burke
1960-1968	Ralph D. Glenn
1968-1972	L. Stanton Dotson
1972-1973	John J. McCarthy
1973-1974	Bobby F. Sanders
1974-1980	Paul C. Komada
1980-1992	Nancy W. Owen
1992-	C. Steve Ferguson

CUMBERLAND COUNTY
JUDGES

Probate Justices of the Peace

1843	Elisha H. Starkweather
1843-1849	James M. Ward

County Judges

1849-1853	James M. Ward
1853-1861	William E. Smith
1861-1864	Hiram B. Decius
1864-1869	Reuben Bloomfield
1869-1873	Wiley Ross
1873-1882	John W. Miller
1882-1886	Leonidas L. Logan
1886-1890	Phillip Welshimer
1890-1894	Leonidas L. Logan

1894-1898	Gershom Monohon
1898-1902	Elias M. McPherson
1902-1906	Stephen B. Rariden
1906-1910	A. L. Ruffner
1910-1917	Stephen B. Rariden
1917-1918	Millard C. Everhart
1918-1930	Albert F. Bussard
1930-1942	Charles M. Connor
1942-1954	Millard C. Everhart
1954-1963	William J. Hill

Associate Judges

1964-1966	William J. Hill
1966-1971	James R. Watson

Circuit Judges

1971-1989	James R. Watson
1990	Thomas M. Burke (recalled)
1990-2002	Robert B. Cochonour
2002-	Millard S. Everhart

STATE'S ATTORNEYS

1872-1876	Andrew J. Lee
1876-1880	Thomas Warner
1880-1884	William C. Prather
1884-1888	Hiram L. Scranton
1888-1896	William H. McDonald
1896-1900	Smith Misner
1900-1904	William H. McDonald
1904-1908	Walter Brewer
1908-1912	Walter C. Greathouse
1912-1915	Walter Brewer
1915-1920	Glenn Ratcliff
1920-1923	Charles C. Eggleston
1923-1928	Walter C. Greathouse
1928-1932	Wilton A. Carr
1932-1940	Theodore O. Cutright
1940-1944	Walter Brewer, Jr.
1944-1952	Glen D. Neal
1952-1956	August C. Caylor
1956-1972	Glen D. Neal
1972-1980	Robert B. Cochonour
1980-1984	Daniel S. Arbogast
1984-1987	Martin R. Schnorf
1987-2002	Millard S. Everhart
2002-	Barry E. Schaefer

EDGAR COUNTY
JUDGES
Judges of Probate

1823-1826	Lewis Murphy
1826-1827	William Lowry
1827-1828	Smith Shaw
1828-1837	Jonathan Mayo

Probate Justices of the Peace

1837-1839	Henry Neville
1839-1849	Samuel Connelly

County Judges

1849-1853	Samuel Connelly
1853-1857	James Steele
1857-1861	A. B. Austin
1861-1865	George K. Larkin
1865-1869	Andrew Y. Trogdon
1869-1877	Robert B. Lamon
1877-1886	Andrew Y. Trogdon
1886-1894	Andrew J. Hunter
1894	Henry Tanner
1894-1898	Erasmus G. Rose
1898-1902	Stephen I. Headley
1902-1910	Walter S. Lamon
1910-1922	Daniel V. Dayton
1922-1946	Paul B. Lauher
1946-1963	Howard T. Ruff

Associate Judges

1964-1971	Howard T. Ruff

Circuit Judges

1971-1972	Howard T. Ruff
1972-1986	Carl A. Lund
1986-2000	Richard E. Scott
2000-2006	H. Dean Andrews
2006-	Steven L. Garst

STATE'S ATTORNEYS

1872-1880	Henry S. Tanner
1880-1888	John W. Shepherd
1888-1892	Frank P. Hardy
1892-1896	Alfred Tanner
1896-1900	Harry H. Van Sellar
1900-1904	John W. Murphy
1904-1908	Walter V. Arbuckle
1908-1912	Richard S. Dyas

1912-1920	Wilber H. Hickman
1920-1924	George W. Bristow
1924-1928	Walter S. Lamon
1928-1932	Charles F. Tym
1932-1936	Walter S. Lamon
1936-1948	Ward E. Dillavou
1948-1952	Wilson Dwyer
1952-1960	Wayne S. Jones
1960-1964	Ralph S. Pearman
1964-1968	Carl A. Lund
1968-1971	Charles J. Gramlich
1971-1976	Arthur A. Jones
1976-1980	Peter T. Dole
1980-1991	Michael M. McFatridge
1992-1996	Allan F. Lolie
1996-2010	Matthew L. Sullivan
2010-	Mark R. Isaf

VERMILION COUNTY
JUDGES
Judges of Probate

1826-1837	Amos Williams

Probate Justices of the Peace

1837-1849	Norman D. Palmer

County Judges

1849-1857	Guy Merrill
1857-1858	Norman D. Palmer
1858-1863	Joseph Peters
1863-1865	Robert B. Lamon
1865-1868	Daniel Clapp
1868-1882	Raymond W. Hanford
1882-1890	David D. Evans
1890-1897	John G. Thompson
1897-1902	Morton W. Thompson
1902-1905	S. Murray Clark
1905-1906	Fred Draper
1906-1909	Isaac A. Love
1909-1918	Lawrence T. Allen
1918-1925	Thomas A. Graham
1925-1930	William T. Henderson
1930-1950	Harlin M. Steely
1950-1962	Frank J. Meyer
1962-1963	James K. Robinson

Associate Judges

1964-1971	James K. Robinson

Circuit Judges

1971-1987	James K. Robinson
1987-1988	Jerry A. Davis
1988-2006	Thomas J. Fahey
2006-	Nancy S. Fahey

Probate Judges

1910-1914	Clinton Abernathy
1914-1930	Walter J. Bookwalter
1930-1938	Ralph M. Jinkins
1938-1954	Arthur R. Hall
1954-1958	John W. Unger
1958-1963	Paul M. Wright

Associate Judges

1964-1971	Paul M. Wright

Circuit Judges

1971-1987	Paul M. Wright
1987-2000	John P. O'Rourke
2000-	Craig H. DeArmond

Circuit Judges

1998-	Michael D. Clary

STATE'S ATTORNEYS

1872-1876	Peter Walsh
1876-1880	Joseph W. Jones
1880-1881	James A. Outland
1881-1884	Charles M. Swallow
1884-1887	William J. Calhoun
1888	John G. Thompson
1888-1892	Hiram P. Blackburn
1892-1900	Seymour G. Wilson
1900-1908	John W. Keeslar
1908-1924	John H. Lewman
1924-1932	Elmer O. Furrow
1932-1940	Oliver D. Mann
1940-1952	William T. Henderson
1952-1956	John T. Allen
1956-1964	John R. Dean
1964-1968	John P. O'Rourke
1968-1969	John Morton Jones

1969-1970	John W. Unger
1970-1972	Everett L. Laury
1972-1976	Richard J. Doyle
1976-1980	Thomas J. Fahey
1980-1984	Edward Litak
1984-1992	Craig H. DeArmond
1992-1998	Michael D. Clary
1998-2000	Larry S. Mills
2000-2008	Frank R. Young
2008-	Randall J. Brinegar

ASSOCIATE JUDGES
Clark, Edgar, and Cumberland Counties

Magistrates

| 1965-1971 | Henri I. Ripstra |

Associate Judges

1971	Henri I. Ripstra
1972-1986	Richard E. Scott
1987-2000	H. Dean Andrews
2001-	David W. Lewis

Coles County

Magistrates

| 1965-1966 | Mark B. Hunt |
| 1966-1971 | Thomas M. Burke |

Associate Judges

1971-1973	Thomas M. Burke
1974-1980	Tom E. Grace
1980-1983	Loren J. Kabbes
1983-1989	Ashton C. Waller
1989-1992	Gary W. Jacobs
1993-1996	Dale A. Cini
1997-2004	Teresa K. Righter
2005-	Brien J. O'Brien

Vermilion County *(three positions)*

Magistrates

1965-1971	John F. Twomey
1965-1971	Matthew A. Jurczak
1967-1971	Lawrence T. Allen, Jr.

Associate Judges

1971-1973	John F. Twomey
1971-1984	Matthew A. Jurczak
1971-1984	Lawrence T. Allen, Jr.

1974-1986	Rita B. Garman
1984-1991	Joseph C. Moore
1984-2010	Joseph P. Skowronski
1987-1995	David G. Bernthal
1991-2009	James K. Borbely
1995-2010	Gordon R. Stipp
1995-1997	Joseph C. Moore (recalled)
2009-	Mark S. Goodwin
2010-	Derek J. Girton
2010-	Karen E. Wall

HIGHER COURTS (local judges)
SUPREME COURT

1873-1893	John Scholfield
1888-1907	Jacob W. Wilkin
1907-1933	Frank K. Dunn
1938-1951	Walter T. Gunn
1951-1961	George W. Bristow
2001-	Rita B. Garman

APPELLATE COURT

1877-1885	Oliver L. Davis
1885-1888	Jacob W. Wilkin
1914-1915	William B. Scholfield
1921-1927	Augustus A. Partlow
1942-1951	George W. Bristow
1951-1955	Ben F. Anderson
1957-1964	John F. Spivey
1985-1991	Joseph R. Spitz
1986-1995	Carl A. Lund
1995-2001	Rita B. Garman

CHIEF JUDGES

1964-1966	Robert F. Cotton, *Paris*
1966-1968	John F. Spivey, *Danville*
1968-1972	Harry I. Hannah, *Mattoon*
1972-1976	Jacob Berkowitz, *Mattoon*
1976-1995	Ralph S. Pearman, *Paris*
1995-2000	Richard E. Scott, *Paris*
2000-2001	James R. Glenn, *Mattoon*
2001-2003	Ashton C. Waller, *Charleston*
2003-2007	James R. Glenn, *Mattoon*
2007-2011	Tracy W. Resch, *Marshall*
2011-	Millard S. Everhart, *Toledo*

PRESIDING JUDGES (1977-)

Clark County

1977-1988	Caslon K. Bennett
1990	James K. Robinson
2004-	Tracy W. Resch

Coles County

1977-1986	William J. Sunderman
1986-1998	Paul C. Komada
1998-2003	Ashton C. Waller
2003-2011	Gary W. Jacobs
2011-	Teresa K. Righter

Cumberland County

1977-1989	James R. Watson
1990	Thomas M. Burke
2002	Tracy W. Resch
2002-	Millard S. Everhart

Edgar County

1977-1998	Ralph S. Pearman
1998-2000	Richard E. Scott
2000-2006	H. Dean Andrews
2006	James R. Glenn
2006-	Steven L. Garst

Vermilion County

1977-1979	Frank J. Meyer
1979-1985	James K. Robinson
1985-1987	Paul M. Wright
1987-1995	Rita B. Garman
1995-2000	John P. O'Rourke
2000-2005	Thomas J. Fahey
2005-2009	Claudia S. Anderson
2009-	Michael D. Clary

ADMINISTRATIVE ASSISTANTS

Secretaries

1964-1966	Mildred P. Weston
1966-1967	Mildred J. Towle

Administrative Secretaries

1967-1968	Mildred J. Towle
1968-1985	Sibyl E. Etchason

Administrative Assistants

1985-1991	Sibyl E. Etchason
1991-2007	Ann E. Staats
2007-	Kathy Lay

SOURCES

Sources listed in "Elections" above; all editions of the *Blue Book of the State of Illinois*; Records of Clark County Circuit Clerk, Terri Reynolds, Coles County Circuit Clerk, Vicki Kirkpatrick, Cumberland County Circuit Clerk, Golda Dunn, Edgar County Circuit Clerk, Karen Halloran, and Vermilion County Circuit Clerk, Dennis R. Gardner, and staff (2010); and the following: William Henry Perrin, ed., *History of Crawford and Clark Counties, Illinois* (Chicago: O. L. Baskin & Co., 1883), 252-253, 256, 283; H. C. Bell, ed., *Clark County* (Chicago: Middle West Publishing Co., 1907), 629-634, 637-640; *The History of Coles County, Illinois* (Chicago: Wm. Le Baron, Jr. & Co., 1879), 245-248; Charles Edward Wilson, ed., *History of Coles County* (Chicago: Munsell Publishing Co., 1906), 677; *History of the City of Mattoon, Illinois*, 45, 46, 51; *Counties of Cumberland, Jasper and Richland, Illinois* (Chicago: F. A. Battey & Co., 1884), 140-142, 147; *The History of Edgar County, Illinois* (Chicago: Wm. Le Baron, Jr. & Co., 1879), 251-253; H. Van Sellar, ed., *History of Edgar County* (Chicago: Munsell Publishing Co., 1905), 660; Lottie E. Jones, *History of Vermilion County, Illinois* (Chicago: Pioneer Publishing Co., 1911), 316, 317, 322-323; John Twomey, ed., *Vermilion County Bench and Bar: The First One Hundred Fifty Years 1826-1976* (Danville: The Vermilion County Bar Association, 1977), 31, 33, 35, 36, 42, 44.

ABOUT THE AUTHOR

James R. Glenn is a circuit judge in the Fifth Judicial Circuit of Illinois, having been elected in 1998. He was the circuit's chief judge from 2003 to 2007. A resident of Mattoon, Glenn graduated in 1982 from the University of Illinois, where he studied political science and history. His interest in politics and history began as a youngster, when his father was the county state's attorney. Glenn is married with three adult children.

INDEX

Cook, Wayne, 51
Cooper, Joseph E., 49
Cooper, Joshua P., 37, 62
Cooper, Thomas M., 33
Cork, Walter E., 36
Cotton, Robert F., 14, 20, 24-25, 31, 57, 61, 66
Cowton, James, 37
Cox, J. C., 48
Craddock, William W., 6, 29, 63
Craig, Harold A., 55
Craig, Isaac B., 10, 38–39, 63
Craig, James W., 9–11, 30–31, 39, 61, 63
Craven, James C., 56
Creighton, James A., 56
Crews, William J., 30
Crose, Ruth E., 20
Crouch, Lloyd, 30
Crum, William H., 37
Cunningham, James R., 5, 29, 37, 39, 60–61, 63
Cunningham, W. C., 37
Cusick, Jay Fay, 47–48
Cutright, Theodore O., 11, 44–45, 64

D

Dalbey, Everett L., 51–52
Davis, Addison N., 50
Davis, David, 4, 29, 59–60
Davis, Jerry A., 52, 55, 65
Davis, John M., 52
Davis, Oliver L., 6-7, 29-30, 59-60, 66
Davis, Thomas D., 39
Davison, M. B., 34, 62
Dayton, Daniel V., 47, 64
Dean, John R., 53–55, 65
DeArmond, Craig H., 21-22, 52, 54, 58, 65-66
Decius, Hiram B., 5, 29–30, 42, 59, 63
Decius, Lyle, 31
Dedman, James C., 41
Delap, M. I., 47

Dennis, Andrew B., 31, 51, 53
Deters, Duane, 41
Devens, Charles J., 54
Dillavou, Ward E., 48–50, 65
Dilsaver, Jewell I., 40, 63
Dixon, S. S., 33
Doak, John W., 48
Dole, Peter T., 49, 65
Donahue, William T., 54–55
Dotson, L. Stanton, 20-22, 40, 63
Douglas, Clarence H., 38, 63
Downey, William H., 35, 62
Doyle, Richard J., 54, 66
Drake, John N., 50
Draper, Fred, 65
Dunbar, Alexander P., 6, 39, 60–61
Dunbar, S. M., 62
Dundas, Frederick W., 31
Dunn, Frank K., 9, 31, 56, 61, 66
Dwyer, William H., 51
Dwyer, Wilson, 49, 65
Dyas, Joseph E., 48
Dyas, Richard S., 48, 64

E

Eads, James A., 29
Eads, Sidney E., 48
Ebdon, Priscilla, 41
Eden, John R., 60
Edmon, Joseph, 37
Edwards, Gideon, 37, 62
Edwards, W. O., 31, 51–52
Eggleston, Charles C., 44, 64
Elder, E. D., 39
Elder, John E., 41
Ellsberry, Bert H., 19
Elsdon, Isaac, 52
Emmerson, Charles, 59
Estes, W. L., 48
Etchason, Sibyl E., 25-27, 67
Evans, David D., 51, 65
Everhart, Millard C., 13, 43, 45, 64

Everhart, Millard S., 13, 27-28, 43, 45, 58, 64, 66-67
Ewart, Herman O., 43
Ewing, C. A., 30

F

Fahey, Nancy S., 18, 22, 52, 55, 65
Fahey, Thomas J., 18, 21, 27-28, 52, 54-55, 58, 65-67
Failing, John K., 48
Ferguson, C. Steve, 17, 32, 40–41, 63
Ficklin, Orlando B., 4, 30, 60–61
Fitzhenry, Louis, 56
Fletcher, Charles H., 38, 40, 63
Foreman, Ray M., 51
Fouts, John J., 46
Fox, Frank E., 47, 49
Fox, Sebastian C., 32
French, Augustus C., 4, 60–61
French, Frank, 19
Fruin, Roger, 47
Fryer, A. J., 37–38
Furrow, Elmer O., 53–55, 65

G

Gano, Kenneth R., 45
Gard, Fred, 34–36
Gard, Jed, 33, 62
Gard, U. R., 33
Garman, Rita B., 16-17, 20-21, 27, 32, 56-58, 61, 66-67
Garst, Steven L., 21, 23, 28, 48-49, 64, 67
Gasaway, Henry, 33, 62
Gill, James, 42
Girton, Derek J., 23, 55, 66
Glenn, James R., 17, 22, 27-28, 32, 58, 61, 66-67, 69
Glenn, Ralph D., 40–41, 63
Godels, Peter P., 20
Goodwin, Mark S., 23, 66
Grace, Tom E., 20-21, 66

Graham, James W., 30
Graham, Thomas A., 51, 54, 65
Gramlich, Charles J., 49, 65
Gray, Orrin J., 19
Gray, Robert M., 39, 63
Greathouse, Walter C., 43–44, 64
Green, D. B., 44
Green, E. B., 30
Green, Edward R., 30
Green, Frederick S., 57
Green, Kenneth A., 38
Griffith, William R., 30, 33, 62
Grisamore, Charles W., 46
Groppi, Gino, 53
Grover, W. C., 33
Gunn, Walter T., 12, 56, 66
Guy, Charles V., 51

H

Hall, Arthur R., 11, 52, 54–55, 65
Hall, Charles C., 17, 52, 55
Hall, John S., 7-8, 39
Halley, John H., 7, 30, 59
Hammond, Robert G., 39–40, 63
Hammond, R. T., 41
Hanford, Raymond W., 50, 65
Hannah, Harry I., 14-15, 20, 24-26, 31-32, 57, 61, 66
Hannah, J. B., 46
Hannold, Samuel F., 47
Harding, G. C., 37
Hardy, Frank P., 48, 64
Hare, Hark D., 34
Harlan, Jacob, 62
Harlan, Justin, 3-5, 29, 33, 59-60, 62
Harper, Jesse, 53
Harrah, John P., 37, 63
Harwood, Hugh, 40, 63
Hasch, H. J., 40–41, 43–44, 55
Hawes, M. D., 50
Hayes, John M., 37
Headley, Stephen I., 47, 64

Hearse, Joseph A., 33
Heinlein, C. M., 40–41, 63
Henderson, William T., 51, 53–55, 65
Henley, F. N., 41
Henley, Lapsley C., 7, 10, 37–38, 63
Herrick, Lott R., 56
Hickman, Robert Z., 56
Hickman, Wilber H., 48, 65
Hicks, Charles E., 45
Hicks, Guy, 47, 49
Hill, C. R., 51
Hill, William J., 13, 25, 43, 45, 64
Hobart, J. R., 37
Hobler, Rick L., 41
Hoff, George S., 51
Hollenbeck, John M., 34–36, 62
Hollenbeck, Lawrence, 36
Hollenbeck, William T., 33, 62
Hoult, C. Howard, 47
Howell, Jason W., 48
Howerton, L. K., 47
Hudson, Jacob J., 39
Hudson, J. F., 33
Hudson, Mac G., 47
Hughes, James F., 10, 30, 38, 59–60, 63
Hunt, Mark B., 20, 66
Hunter, Andrew J., 5, 31, 46–47, 64
Hutchinson, T. W., 30
Hutchison, D. S., 42
Hutton, H. Ernest, 55

I

Icenogle, Carus S., 38
Isaf, Mark R., 49, 65

J

Jacobs, Gary W., 21-22, 28, 39, 41, 58, 63, 66-67
Janney, Harry M., 33, 62
Jeter, George M., 47
Jewell, W. R., 54

Jinkins, Ralph M., 10-11, 52, 54, 65
Jinkins, Samuel V., 52, 55
Johnson, Dillard N., 8, 48
Johnson, Grant, 48, 50
Jones, Arthur A., 21, 49, 65
Jones, Edmund D., 34, 62
Jones, Edwin D., 33
Jones, James P., 62
Jones, John Morton, 15, 54, 65
Jones, Joseph W., 52, 65
Jones, J. T., 56
Jones, Wayne S., 49–50, 65
Jones, William C., 7, 30, 59
Jurczak, Matthew A., 16, 20-21, 61, 66

K

Kabbes, Loren J., 21, 66
Kannmacher, Frederick, 34
Kash, Richard M., 45
Keeslar, John W., 53, 65
Kelley, A., 42
Kelly, James A., 33
Kerby, Robert B., 19
Kidwell, William K., 38, 40, 63
Kiger, Carl D., 40
Kimbrough, E. R. E., 9, 31, 61
Kime, David O., 19
Kincaid, John T., 10–11, 37–39, 41, 63
Kincaid, Stewart W., 48
Kingsbury, Arius A., 56
Kitchell, Alfred, 29, 60–61
Kleinfelter, L. F., 47
Komada, Paul C., 15, 17, 20, 27, 32, 40-41, 58, 61, 63, 67
Kreckman, Fred, 32

L

Lakey, Randy A., 54
Lambright, John A., 51–52, 54
Lamon, Robert B., 5, 46, 50, 64–65
Lamon, Walter S., 5, 47-48, 50, 64-65